To my daughter Laura, the best art director I know

To my son Matteo, my best consultant

To my husband Maurizio, for sharing his patience,
affection and competence with me when I am
endeavouring to write a book

To my assistant, Carolina Alvarado Camero,
for her professionalism and efficiency combined
with creativity and a sense of elegance

DEANNA FARNETI CERA

COPPOLA E TOPPO FASHION JEWELLERY

ANTIQUE COLLECTORS' CLUB

ACKNOWLEDGEMENTS

Project Coordinator: Marco Jellinek
Editor: Susannah Hecht
Translator: Ettore Mazza
Design and layout: John and Orna Designs, London
Colour separation: Antique Collectors' Club, Woodbridge, Suffolk

Printed in China for the Antique Collectors' Club Ltd, Woodbridge, Suffolk

I am deeply indebted to Gian Paolo Barbieri for the honour of allowing me to use his wonderful pictures of Coppola e Toppo jewels worn by stunning models, a combination which further generates beauty and class. I want to thank him and his assistant, Emmanuele Randazzo, also for the patience with which they met all my requests.

I am grateful to everybody who joined me in making this enjoyable project, particularly those who loaned pieces: Barbara Berger, Mexico City; Leila Marzagao, London; Ginger Moro, Los Angeles; Gian Paolo Barbieri, Irma Barni Castiglioni, Paola Bay, Maura Caminada, Enrica Cibulli, Pupa (Maria Cristina) Coppola, Luisa Gregoriani, Marina Gregotti, Mania Huska, Anna Negrisoli Bellora, Donatella Pellini, Maria Pia and Alessandro Rossi Unger, Milan; Carolle Thibaut Pomerantz Chastagnol, Marion Stern, Paris; Enrico Quinto, Rome; Chisa Kotaki, Tokyo; as well as all those who preferred to remain anonymous.

This book would not have seen the light of day without the unconditional approval of my publishers, Diana Steel of Antique Collectors' Club (Woodbridge) and Marco Jellinek of Officina Libraria (Milan): their staff, and in particular Susannah Hecht, Senior Editor of Antique Collectors' Club and Paola Gallerani at Officina Libraria, have made a fundamental contribution to the success of this book.

A crucial mention also for Yoox, in particular Holly Bruback, their creative consultant, who believed in this book since its beginning and encouraged me through the difficulties and obstacles to get it done. Condé Nast Italy, particularly Paola Raineri and Claudia Marra of the Central Library of Milan, have helped me to research old images, articles and archive prints, for which I am extremely grateful.

Pippo Ansaldo shared his expertise as Art Director by giving helpful initial suggestions for the layout of the book.

Giulia Martinetti and Mina Lucchini from Milan, who worked for many years for Coppola e Toppo, have dug deep in their memories to help reconstruct Lyda's Coppola life and career.

A warm thank you also to the antique dealers of vintage jewellery and dresses who have contributed to help put together this collection of jewellery by Coppola e Toppo, offering me the best available on the market and daring sometimes to ask their customers to lend their Coppola pieces in order to be photographed for this book: Brett Benson, Chicago; Andrea Zucchi, Florence; William Wain, London; Alessandra Chiodi and Claudia Jesi (Cavalli e Nastri), Milan; Bonny Yaukauer, New Jersey; Pauline Gasbarro, Barbara Owen and Clair Watson, New York; Antonella Grammatico from "Per Lei" and Anouk Barletta, Paris; Lee Caplan, Toronto; Ingrid Hofstätter, Vienna.

Finally, much of the enthusiasm and engagement necessary to put together this book came from the encouragement and closeness of some of my friends and students, who very often acted as researchers/gofers, helping with anything that was needed: Stefania Bertaglia, Cristina Castillo, Roberta Della Penna, Veronica Guiduzzi, Luciana Silvestri, Alessandra Scotti, Renzo Tabellini, Ines Tejada, and Francesco Tridente.

Previous spread: This photograph of Veruschka wearing the arrow-shaped necklace by Coppola e Toppo was chosen as the poster for the exhibition dedicated to Gian Paolo Barbieri by the municipality of Milan (Palazzo Reale, 19 September - 11 November 2007)

CONTENTS

A portrait of Bruno and Lyda Coppola
by Gian Paolo Barbieri, 1965

FOREWORD

"THE BASIC RULE WITH JEWELS IS 'TOO MUCH DEFORMS'. YOU CAN GO AS FAR AS YOU LIKE IN REGARDS
TO THE STRENGTH OF THE PIECE, THE ORIGINALITY OF THE DESIGN, THE COLOUR, BUT NEVER IN QUANTITY.
TOO MANY JEWELS ARE GOOD FOR A CIRCUS PARADE, BUT DO NOT MAKE YOU LOOK ELEGANT."

As luck would have it, in December 1987, I came across a sizeable collection of Coppola e Toppo jewellery being mounted in the showroom at Finarte, an auction house in Milan, where my husband works. Ultimately held on 12 December, it was actually the first auction in Italy dedicated to fashion accessories and was second only to the fashion jewellery auction at Sotheby's, New York on 21 October 1987, which had showcased the collection of Diana Vreeland, the legendary director of *Vogue America,* and later consultant at the Costume Department of the Metropolitan Museum.

On that day in December I was struck and fascinated by the objects on display for a variety of reasons: their diversity compared to the fashion jewellery I had seen until then (endowed, in any case, with clearcut features), the evocative power of the colours, the wealth of shapes and motifs, the multitude of materials used. At that time I was not really as familiar with Italian ornaments, as I was with American fashion jewellery, having supervised, just a few months earlier, the catalogue and selection of items to be put on display at the successful exhibition 'Le gioie di Hollywood' held at the Venice Design Art Gallery in Venice from February to May 1987.

As I gradually browsed the nearly 150 articles destined for auction, a significant sample of the works of Coppola e Toppo, I could sense the start of a real passion developing for those pieces of jewellery and the need to better understand the artist behind such particular ornaments. From that day on, the name of their designer, Lyda Coppola, has always been present in the research that, over a period of twenty years, has enabled me to accumulate sufficient information to attempt, with this book, a reconstruction of her creative path.

French *Vogue*, May 1948, p.19
dedicated to the jewellery of Lyda Coppola

"YOU CAN WEAR FINE JEWELS ONLY WHEN YOU GO TO THE OPENING OF *LA SCALA* OR AT A WEDDING. FOR ANY OTHER OCCASION, IT'S BETTER TO LEAVE THEM IN THE VAULT, TO FORGET THEM, ESPECIALLY THE PEARL NECKLACE. ANY WOMAN WEARING IT LOOKS AUTOMATICALLY TWENTY YEARS BEHIND THE TIMES."

When asked the question "Was it difficult at first to get your jewellery known?", Lyda Coppola, in an interview in 1971, answered:

"Very much so. In fact, when I started out, and for many years after, I was quite unknown in Italy. I had, instead, immediately achieved some success in Paris, but that was almost to be expected. Paris was the city of fashion jewellery. In order to find out if I was doing the right thing, I decided to go to France and show my creations. In that period, 1948, Paris was the place where copies of real jewels were being made and that was exactly the thing I had never wanted to do.

In any case, I decided one day to take a handful of my latest designs (packed in a very small suitcase because it was illegal then to export jewels) and, having arrived in Paris, I showed up at *Vogue*. An extremely kind lady, Madame Sweetenbourgh, unwrapped my bundle and then stared at my jewellery with a blank look on her face; without uttering a word, she got up, took my jewellery and left the room. It seemed an eternity but she was only gone about ten minutes, and then she reappeared in the company of a rather small and bald man who, without beating about the bush, asked me if I had really created those pieces of jewellery. Then he asked me to follow him; they were finishing a feature about fashion accessories and they had found my jewellery to be so beautiful and original that, if I agreed, they would immediately photograph them. I worked all day and night with their photographer, and the result was that French *Vogue* published every one of those pieces of jewellery I had brought with me, on a two-page colour spread.[1]

That bald and not very tall man happened to be the editor of French *Vogue*. He gave me the addresses of the most important French couturiers and letters of presentation. That's how my wonderful adventure with fashion jewellery began"[2]

It was to be an adventure that lasted a lifetime, one in which Lyda Coppola saw her company trademark associated with the leading personalities in French and Italian fashion.

[1] Le point de vue de Vogue, French *Vogue*, May 1948, p.19 (author's note: It was a single page in b/w and not two pages in colour)
[2] Fogliani P., 'Con perline e cristalli ho conquistato il mondo' in *Oggi*, Milan, 16 September 1971, pp.66-71

LE
POINT
DE VUE
DE VOGUE

Hier, VOGUE s'est attaché à résumer les tendances de la mode nouvelle : à définir le style de son architecture. Aujourd'hui relevant les détails qui ajoutent à sa ligne, énumérant ces mille riens charmants issus de la boutique du couturier, il apparaît que l'accessoire est devenu indispensable. Pas plus qu'elle ne sortirait sans fard, une femme ne quitterait son boudoir sans fixer à sa taille, agrafer à son col, faire jaillir de sa manche ce mouchoir, cette touffe de fleurs qui font chanter sa robe. Au talent du créateur qui propose, elle répond par le choix qui dispose : par une intelligence de sa beauté aussi subtile que celle dite, en amour, intelligence du cœur. De l'étoile qu'elle fixe en ses cheveux aux liens nouant sa cheville, une femme se doit, parmi les détails où se complaît sa fantaisie, de lucidement soupeser, jauger, comparer, éliminer, imposer : qu'elle sache d'instinct ou laisse guider son geste, qu'elle accepte ou décide, son élégance est fonction de son choix.

Bijoux de Madame COPPOLA TOPPO.
Le collier de droite a été créé pour Robert Piguet.
Photo Des Russell.

"THE MORE IMPORTANT THE JEWEL IS, THE MORE IT NEEDS TO STAND ALONE."

Lyda Coppola was born in Venice, during the great war, on 26 March in 1915. Her father originated from Torino while her mother – a member of the important Jewish family, Cantoni – came from Trieste with Neapolitan ancestors. After successfully obtaining her high-school diploma, she attended the Academy of Fine Arts in Venice for just two years. Up until 1938, she had tried her hand in a variety of fields without really finding anything that had captured her interest. She was drawn to art and modern sculpture, and she had always been interested in classical music (her mother was a piano teacher and her uncle a composer). Though she would have liked to have become a doctor or an aviator, unable to achieve this, she settled for a training course to become a Red Cross nurse.

Unfulfilled, and in the hopes of turning her creative aspirations into reality, she decided to leave the family home and move to Milan on her own. During those difficult war years, she worked as a clerk and as a bookkeeper. Then, with the war finally over, she was able to embark on a career as a designer with the fashion house Braito – Giunta. In her spare time, she was being taught how to make costume jewellery by Ada Politzer, a Czechoslovakian Jewish refugee. Politzer was able to survive this harsh period by creating jewellery in her small apartment with a supply of stones she had taken with her when she had escaped from her country.

In 1946, Lyda married Ferruccio Toppo, a well-off manager. With this change in her personal life, she decided also to abandon her career of designer and start up her own business, convinced that her passion for art, nature and music, together with her sharp sense of methodical and never-ending observation of all that lay around her, would provide the support in creating unusual and elegant objects. For the next two years Lyda could afford the luxury of not having to work for anyone and she made costume jewellery to satisfy her taste using diverse and typically Italian materials such as Torre del Greco coral and Venetian *conterie* (smooth glass pierced beads, which have been made in Venice since 1300). Although the marriage was not perfect – Ferruccio found it difficult to settle down as a married man – Lyda remained devoted to her husband for the rest of her life.

Lyda was particularly close to her brother Bruno (Trieste 1914 – Milan 2007), who had been a pilot in the Air Force during the war. Struck by the beauty of Lyda's

il comandante
brunetta

3 M. A., 'Il giro del mondo in ottanta minuti' in *La Scala*, *Rivista dell'opera*, May 1958, p.59
4 Fogliani P., *ibid*

Necklace, earrings and bracelet, no. 90,
ordered in 1948 by Jeanne Lanvin
Bruno Coppola archives, Milan

Necklace and earrings model 80, 1948
Bruno Coppola archives, Milan

Necklaces, models 72 and 73, 1948
Bruno Coppola archives, Milan

creations, he took a small range of samples to a friend, the owner of a fashion accessory shop in Via Condotti in Rome; he bought the lot!

It was Bruno who convinced Lyda to dedicate herself full time to fashion jewellery, an innovative sector, in his opinion, and perfectly suited to his sister's creative personality. In 1948 two workers joined Lyda and Bruno, and they decided to try their fortune in Paris. Carrying a small suitcase full of items they set of for Paris to show to the legendary French experts Lyda's work; the response was better than expected or even hoped for.

After two years of working together, in 1950 Bruno and Lyda were finally in a position to put their business on a legal footing and formally founded the company Coppola e Toppo, which was based at 4 Via Morelli, Milan. Bruno worked alongside Lyda as marketing and business manager, a role he kept for the rest of his working life.

The workshop and showroom took up the top floor of a Milanese period house, with a window looking out on to a tiny roof terrace covered in ivy clinging all the way up to the roofs of the neighbouring houses. A fashion journalist in 1958 recalls her visit to the Coppola e Toppo showroom: "Lyda Toppo and Bruno Coppola cautiously half-open an old jewellery box and warily remove the pieces ready for America which will be seen in Italy only next year... the colour atlas of faceted crystal beads inundate the room with light, releasing a multitude of little flickering stars on the walls and on the ceiling. The colours most favoured are beaver, pastel mink and silver blue mink, burnt gold, the full range of ruby reds, steel, black, smoke-grey, *sleeping blue*, three shades of sapphire, storm green and stream green".[3]

The name chosen for the business, Coppola e Toppo (Lyda and Bruno's surname combined with that of Lyda's husband) was, in Lyda's own words, "an absurd, ridiculous name… but fun. Once memorised, it's never forgotten".[4]

Collar necklace, c.1949
Simulated pearls weft-mounted and interspersed
with coral spheres and branches

Collar necklace with side horseshoe motif, c.1950
String-mounted and pavé-embroidered glass paste
faceted beads interspersed with small gilded spheres

Demi-parure made up of necklace and bracelet, late 1940s
Glass paste spheres simulating turquoise, half-crystal faceted
beads and simulated pearls strung and mounted in a pavé
embroidery on the clasp

WHY FASHION JEWELLERY?

"IT IS ALWAYS NECESSARY TO CREATE A SEPARATION, AN EMPTY SPACE BETWEEN ONE JEWEL AND
ANOTHER. WHEN THE NECKLACE MAKES A STATEMENT, NO EARRINGS; WHEN THE EARRING IS IMPORTANT,
NO NECKLACE, MAYBE A BRACELET."

Lyda chose fashion jewellery rather than fine jewellery, because she felt that accessories should be developed alongside the dress which they were meant to complement. "I was fed up with seeing women decked out like the Virgin Mary of Loreto: gold, silver, pearls and diamonds worn like votive statues. And, even worse, everyone looked the same, without a hint of originality. I created fashion jewellery to give women the possibility of being different, one from another. In order to do this, there was just one way: eliminate the kind of jewellery that everyone possessed in quantity; there was a need for more colourful jewellery, more visible, more modern, definitely more personal, and, above all each piece had to be made for a certain outfit. In my opinion, it was absurd, even grotesque to imagine that a piece of jewellery made fifty years before could be associated with a modern dress".[5]

When asked why she felt that fine jewellery did not express personality and was not modern, she responded: "Because, whether it is made of gold, diamonds or pearls, the classic piece of jewellery is insufficiently colourful, small in size, almost identical in workmanship. In short, it's like a uniform. What a depressing sight! I was able to verify this many years ago at a reception one evening. I had a look round and saw that the women there, all of them, wore little black dresses with two or three strands of pearls, real of course; a diamond brooch, real of course; a bracelet in solid or light gold. They didn't look like women at all but just a bunch of mannequins all dressed and bejewelled in the same manner. They looked like the students of an all-girls' school, all with their nameplates well in view. They had a lot going for them, but they had no personality. What personality can a real piece of jewellery express, when, inevitably, it's limited in shape, in cut and in colour? It's valuable, that's what it is. But the value of an object doesn't express the personality of the individual wearing it. It can only show that the person is rich, and you're not going to tell me that only rich people have personality".[6]

[5] Fogliani P., *ibid*
[6] Fogliani P., *ibid*

Three-strand necklace with central cameo
for Edward Molyneux, 1949
Graduating simulated pearls, old turtleshell
cameo mounted on brass pendant/clasp, conterie
Published in *Bellezza*, January 1949, p.146

"WHEN THE OUTFIT IS IMPORTANT, NEVER LOAD IT DOWN WITH JEWELS. ONE ONLY, BUT CLASSY, IS ENOUGH."

Coming back to the article that appeared in French *Vogue* in 1948, it is almost miraculous that experts such as the editorial staff of the most famous fashion magazine in the world should have chosen a few necklaces created by Lyda Coppola, an unknown Italian, to assert how costume jewellery had become essential on the fashion scene as an expression of elegance and personality. It should be pointed out that materials such as red coral and crystal beads in a multitude of shades – from turquoise to water green, from purple to straw yellow – used in Coppola e Toppo jewellery hark back to the notion, so dear to foreigners and Americans in particular, that Italy is the land of sunshine and holidays, of art and excellent cuisine.

With the unexpected and extraordinary success that came with the page on *Vogue*, the French *couturiers* wasted no time in placing their first orders: in 1948 Jeanne Lanvin and Robert Piguet purchased an interesting number of pieces from the Coppolas, choosing from various models and ordering one or two specimens of each. In November 1949 French *Vogue* dedicated another colour page to Coppola e Toppo fashion jewellery. In that same year, Jacques Fath chose Lyda's jewellery to accompany his collections, while in the following year orders arrived from Pierre Balmain, Jacques Griffe, Nina Ricci, Cristobal Balenciaga, Edward Molyneux, Jacques Heim, Elsa Schiaparelli, as well as Christian Dior, with whom Coppola e Toppo collaborated until his death in 1957. The company archives reveal that the *couturiers* were sweeping in their choice of models but were extremely cautious when it came to quantity, never ordering beyond two of each type.

The order sheets preserved in the Coppola e Toppo archives provide brief descriptions of the jewellery requested. Today, in the absence of the original pieces (which are almost impossible to find on the antiques market), these short descriptions offer the opportunity to picture what they looked like: "*1 collier jade et corail, 1 collier blanc et 4 motifs corail, 1 collier perles et grenades, boucles d'oreille perles bleu et corail*".[7]

It was Elsa Schiaparelli above all who favoured Coppola e Toppo jewellery and for over five years they were her preferred suppliers. We read in a Schiaparelli order: "*2 colliers cristal de roche, 2 colliers demi lune, 2 broches corail et malachite*" and in another "*3 colliers ceramique vert marron*".[8]

Lyda struck up a lasting friendship with Elsa Schiaparelli, as her words testify: "Everytime I arrived in Paris, there was always a gift waiting for me – her latest perfume. It was Madame Schiaparelli herself who opened the gates to the United States for me. She introduced me to the buyer from Lord & Taylor of New York, who in turn arranged for me to meet Dorothy Shaver, the Chairman of that company which had forty-eight department stores in different American cities".[9]

Evidence of the close relationship between Coppola e Toppo and the Schiaparelli fashion house can be seen by the large press coverage that appeared in the most important fashion magazines of the time, dedicated to Schiaparelli outfits and fashion jewellery, both defined as by Schiaparelli. The reality is that the jewellery pieces were indeed Coppola e Toppo creations, but, as is customary when the client is an important couturier, only his/her trademark appears on the piece of jewellery while the name of the craftsman who works for him/her remains unknown.[10] This is still as true today as it was in the past.

1951 saw a sudden and unexpected change in style for Coppola e Toppo: the rigid embroidered central motif, that had characterized Coppola e Toppo fashion jewellery from the start were replaced with ornaments that were entirely embroidered. According to Vivienne Becker,[11] it was Serge Matta, an assistant of Elsa Schiaparelli and brother of the famous Chilean painter Roberto Echaurren Matta, who designed the first pieces made entirely of beads embroidered on to a rigid metal plate for Coppola e Toppo. I have not been able to confirm this, either from members of the Coppola family or from the period French, Italian and American magazines, that widely reviewed Coppola e Toppo fashion jewellery. However, I am inclined to believe that someone who was used to giving shape to Elsa Schiaparelli's artistic bent did effectively provide Lyda with the initial input to adopt these extraordinary rigid models, particularly innovative when compared to the more traditional and conformist ornamental objects of the time.

[7] Order from Jacques Fath, 28 July, 1949
[8] Orders from Schiaparelli, dated 20 July 1949 and 26 August 1949
[9] Fogliani., *ibid*
In 1945, Dorothy Shaver was the first woman to become President of a department store as important as Lord & Taylor, after managing to establish it as "The name in American style". She was the pioneer for young designers that had arisen – especially in New York – during the period which included the Second World War (Clare Potter, Ruth Payne, Alice Smith, Muriel King, Elizabeth Hawes etc.).
[10] French *Vogue*, November 1949, p.40 and May 1951, pp. 73 and 76
[11] Becker, V., *Fabulous Fakes*, Grafton Books, 1988, p.105

Necklaces, brooches and hair ornaments created
by Coppola e Toppo for Elsa Schiaparelli, 1949
French *Vogue*, November 1949, p.40

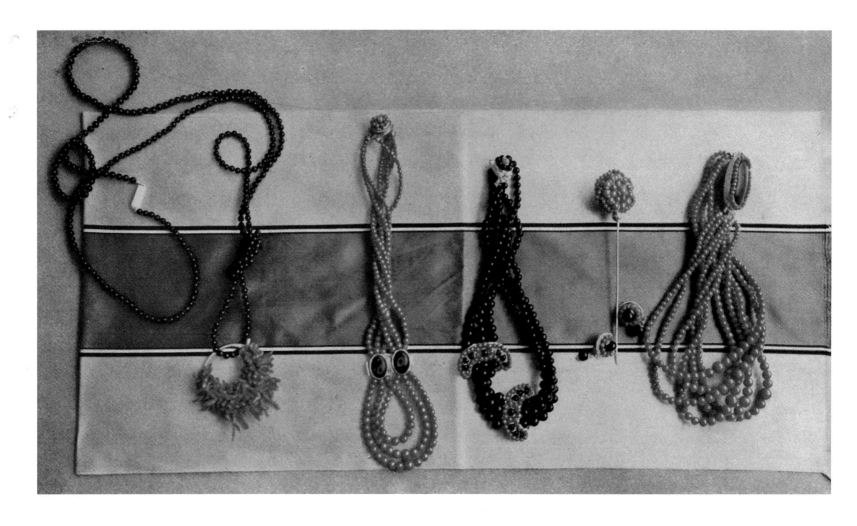

Five-strand graduating necklace, 1949,
belonging to the collection photographed for
French *Vogue*, November 1949, p.40
Graduating glass paste spheres simulating coral,
clasp in malachite surrounded by coral spheres

Three-strand necklace for Elsa Schiaparelli, 1949
String-mounted glass paste spheres simulating
turquoise alternated with coral beads and pavé-
embroidered coral branches and spheres
Marked on brass clasp: *CT* Made in Italy
The necklace is probably part of the collection of
Coppola e Toppo fashion jewellery published by
French *Vogue*, November 1949, p.40

Two-strand necklace for Elsa Schiaparelli, 1949
String-mounted glass paste spheres simulating lapis lazuli
and pavé – embroidered coral branches and spheres
Marked on brass clasp: Made Italy
The necklace is probably part of the collection of
Coppola e Toppo fashion jewellery published by
French *Vogue*, November 1949, p.40

Three-strand necklace with central motif
for Elsa Schiaparelli, c.1949
String-mounted glass paste faceted beads and
coral branches embroidered on the clasp

One-strand collar necklace with cornucopia-shaped motif, c. 1949
Gilded brass and pavé-embroidered coral beads interspersed with brass faceted spacers
Marked: *CT*

23

Considering the extraordinary results of these designs, Lyda was then able to develop this idea by continuing to create pieces of embroidered jewellery that can be defined as small masterpieces of artistic craftsmanship.

From the very start of its activities, Coppola e Toppo was not just limiting itself to the creation of fashion jewellery. Lyda Coppola had, in fact, discovered the possibility of making dress trimmings using crystal beads. In the 1950s she made boleros with glass stones for Sorelle Fontana in Rome and in the early 1960s for Biki and de Barentzen. Lyda even made a few dresses in half-crystal beads – one of which still survives today – and embellishments for umbrella handles, bags and belts, boxes, makeup compacts and shoe buckles.

Demi-parure made up of necklace and
bracelet for Jacques Fath, c.1949
String-mounted half-crystal faceted beads
and pavé-embroidered on rigid central motif,
brass faceted spacers, clasps and bead caps
Marked: Made Italy

Collar necklace and dangling earrings for Jacques Fath, 1949
String-mounted and pavé-embroidered simulated pearls with garnets
also pavé-embroidered on three half-moon shape elements
Marked: Made Italy
Necklace: Pauline Gasbarro Collection, New York
Earrings: Lee Caplan Collection, Toronto

Four-strand necklace for Jacques Fath, c.1950
String-mounted simulated pearls and pavé-
embroidered half-crystal faceted beads on
a V-shaped centre, conterie
Marked on clasp: Made in Italy

Necklaces, brooch and hair ornament
for Elsa Schiaparelli, c.1950
Ginger Moro archives, Los Angeles

Brooch for Elsa Schiaparelli, c.1950
String-mounted simulated pearls, pavé-embroidered
pure crystal faceted beads with brass faceted spacers
and bead caps

VOGUE

LES MARIÉES • LES ROBES LÉGÈRES • LES BLOUSES
SIX CROISIÈRES D'ÉTÉ

MAI 1951 • REVUE MENSUELLE IMPRIMÉE EN FRANCE • 500 FRANCS

Two-strand necklace with central circle
motif propped up by two bridge-shaped
elements for Elsa Schiaparelli, 1950
String-mounted and pavé-embroidered
half-crystal faceted beads, conterie
Marked: Made in Italy by Coppola e Toppo
Published on the cover by French *Vogue*,
May 1951

Model wearing an Elsa Schiaparelli outfit with
a Coppola e Toppo necklace and bracelet
French *Vogue*, May 1951, p.76 (captioned: "by Schiaparelli")

Double-layered necklace for Elsa Schiaparelli, 1951
Glass paste spheres with two rigid metal plate side motifs
overlapped by an embroidery of three rings of coral
spheres, linked by six strands of glass paste spheres
Marked: CᴇT Made in Italy
The same model, made with different materials,
was published in French *Vogue*, May 1951, p.76
Bonny Yankauer Collection, New Jersey

The Schiaparelli boutique in a Brunetta drawing showing two dresses and respective necklaces with rigid elements created by Coppola e Toppo
Primavera – Rivista dell'alta moda (Primavera – High Fashion magazine), no.52, spring 1952, p.71

Rigid necklace for Elsa Schiaparelli, first half of the 1950s
Pavé embroidered half-crystal faceted beads, conterie
Marked: Made in Italy by Coppola e Toppo
Published in P.G. Zucco, 'Coppola e Toppo, pionieri del "Made in Italy" ' in *Or*, December 1991, p.120

Five-strand necklace, c.1951
String-mounted and pavé-embroidered half-crystal
faceted beads and simulated pearls, conterie
Marked: Made in Italy by Coppola e Toppo
William Wain Collection, London

Necklace with V-shaped rigid motifs for Jacques Fath, c.1951
String-mounted simulated round pearls and pavé-embroidered
half-crystal faceted beads, conterie
Marked: Made in Italy by Coppola e Toppo

Demi-parure made up of choker and
bracelet, probably for Jacques Fath, c. 1951
String-mounted half-crystal faceted beads
and simulated baroque pearls, pavé-
embroidery on the clasps
Marked: Made in Italy by Coppola e Toppo

Three-strand necklace, with one pendant
at the front and one at the back, c.1950
String mounted and pavé-embroidered
half-crystal faceted beads
Carolle Thibaut Pomerantz Collection, Paris

V-shaped Indian bracelet for Elsa Schiaparelli, 1952
Pavé-embroidered half-crystal faceted beads
Marked: Made in Italy by Coppola e Toppo
Published in American *Vogue*,
15 November 1952, p.99

Wing-shaped rigid necklace for Elsa Schiaparelli, 1952
Pavé-embroidered half-crystal faceted beads, conterie
Marked: Made in Italy by Coppola e Toppo
Published in Farneti Cera, D. (ed.) *Jewels of fantasy*,
Harry N. Abrams, New York, 1992, p. 279

Five-strand necklace, c.1950
String-mounted glass paste spheres simulating
turquoise and half-crystal faceted beads with
pavé-embroidery on rectangular clasp

Five-strand graduating necklace, c.1950
String-mounted glass paste spheres simulating lapis
lazuli and pavé-embroidered on the rectangular clasp

Two-strand necklace with central rigid motif, c.1951
Glass paste spheres simulating turquoise and citrine,
the former string-mounted and the latter
pavé-embroidered in the central part and in the
clasp, brass faceted bead caps and spacers
Marked: Made Italy

Sautoir with leaf-shaped pendant, c.1951
String-mounted glass paste spheres simulating
jade and pavé-embroidered central pendant,
brass faceted bead caps and spacers
Marked: *C T* Made in Italy

Four-strand bracelet, c.1950
String mounted glass paste spheres simulating
turquoise and pavé-embroidered interspersed
with gilded 'boules' and French wire on the clasp

Three-strand necklace, c.1951
String-mounted glass paste spheres simulating
turquoise and pure crystal faceted beads
Marked: Made in Italy by Coppola e Toppo

Five-strand necklace with central bow motif, c. 1952
String-mounted simulated pearls, pavé-embroidered half-
crystal faceted beads on bow-shaped brass plate, conterie
Marked on the clasp: Made in Italy
Marked on the knot: Made in Italy by Coppola e Toppo

Three-strand collar necklace, c.1950
String-mounted half-crystal faceted beads
and pavé-embroidered on central motif
with incorporated brass clasp
Marked: CεT

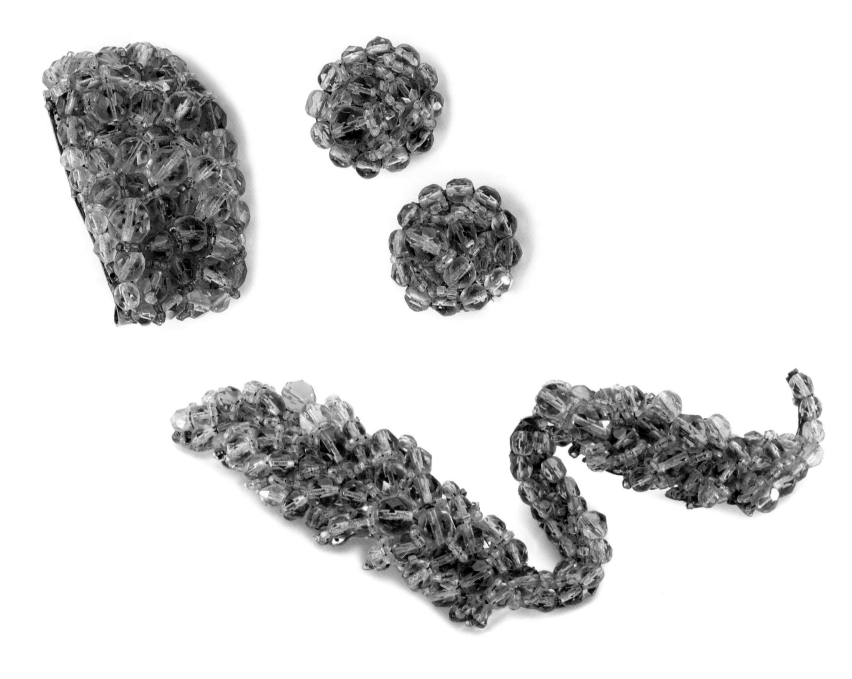

Three-strand necklace with central
rectangular motif with tassels, 1949
String-mounted half-crystal faceted beads and
central motif with incorporated brass clasp
overlapped by pavé embroidery, conterie
Marked: Made in Italy by Coppola e Toppo

Three-strand bracelet, c.1951
Glass paste spheres, some of which
are simulating lapis lazuli and jade,
string and pavé-embroidered
interspersed with brass faceted
bead caps and spacers
Marked: CεT

Single-strand necklace with a rigid central motif, c.1951
String-mounted and pavé-embroidered glass paste spheres
Marked: Made in Italy by Coppola e Toppo

51

Six-strand simulated pearl choker, c.1950
String-mounted simulated pearls with two weft-mounted side motifs in half-crystal faceted beads and pavé-embroidered central motif. Clasp made up with pavé-embroidered faceted glass beads
Marked: Made in Italy by Coppola e Toppo
Published on a Carosa dress in *La Moda*, special issue on the *Rassegna della Ricostruzione Italiana* (Review of the Italian Reconstruction), July 1953, p.30
Chisa Kotaki Collection, Tokyo

Five-strand necklace, early 1950s
String-mounted graduated half-crystal faceted beads with a central drop pendant attached to the clasp, both pavé-embroidered, conterie
Marked: Made in Italy by Coppola e Toppo
Published in Gordon A., *Twentieth Century Costume Jewelry*, Adasia International, 1990, p. 109

The model is wearing the single-strand necklace
with rigid central motifs shown below, c.1952
Ginger Moro archives, Los Angeles

Single-strand necklace with rigid central motifs
(as seen on the model opposite), 1952
String and pavé-embroidered half-crystal faceted beads
Marked: Made in Italy
Pauline Gasbarro Collection, New York

55

Necklace with central pendant, early 1950s
String-mounted simulated pearls in graduating
sizes, pavé-embroidered pendant made up of
half-crystal faceted beads
Marked: Made Italy
Paola Bay Collection, Milan

Two-strand necklace with central leaf motifs, early 1950s
String-mounted and pavé-embroidered half-crystal faceted beads
Marked: Made in Italy

Opposite top left: Slave bracelet, early 1950s
Pavé and 'tuft' style-embroidered half-crystal faceted beads
Marked: Made in Italy by Coppola e Toppo

Opposite bottom left: Cuff bracelet, possibly for
Elsa Schiaparelli, early 1950s
Pavé-embroidered half-crystal faceted beads
Marked: Made in Italy
Barbara Berger Collection, Mexico City

Opposite top right: Indian bracelet, early 1950s
Pavé-embroidered half-crystal faceted beads, conterie
Marked: Made in Italy by Coppola e Toppo

Opposite bottom right: Slave bracelet, early 1950s
Pavé-embroidered half-crystal faceted beads, conterie
Marked: Made in Italy by Coppola e Toppo

Top right: Indian bracelet, early 1950s
Pavé-embroidered half-crystal faceted beads, conterie
Marked: Made in Italy by Coppola e Toppo

Bottom right: Circle brooch overlapped by
a bridge-shaped element, c.1949
Pavé-embroidered half-crystal faceted beads,
brass bead caps and spacers
Marked: Made Italy

Collar necklace, c.1952
String-mounted half-crystal faceted beads and
pavé-embroidered on two rigid side
motifs and one central motif, conterie
Marked: Made in Italy by Coppola e Toppo
Bonny Yankauer Collection, New Jersey

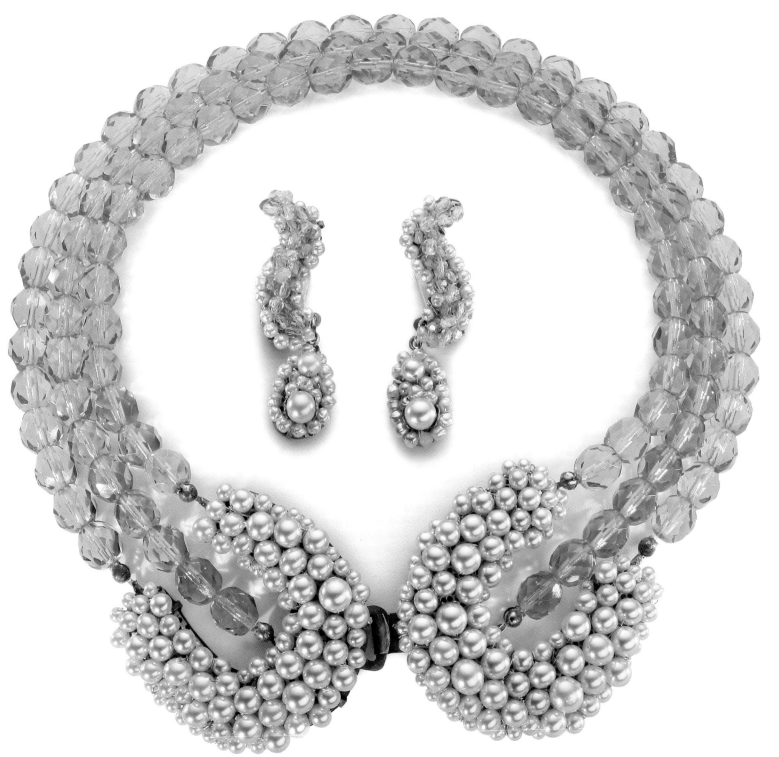

Demi-parure made up of collar necklace and dangling
earrings, early 1950s
String-mounted half-crystal faceted beads and pavé-
embroidered simulated pearls on two rigid horseshoe motifs
Marked: Made in Italy by Coppola e Toppo

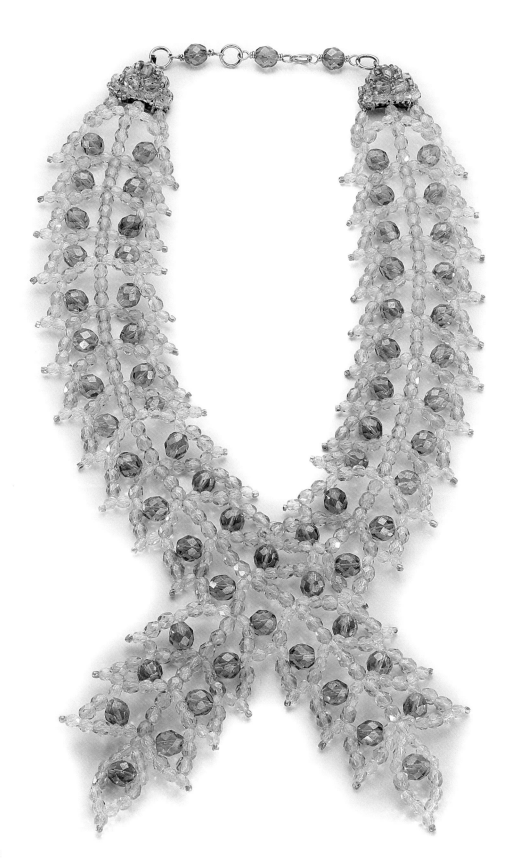

Criss-cross necklace with leaf motifs, early 1950s
Half-crystal faceted beads string-mounted to form
a leaf motif and pavé-embroidered on the heart-
shaped clasp
Marked: Made in Italy by Coppola e Toppo

Necklace with a rigid central criss-cross
motif, early 1950s
String-mounted and pavé-embroidered
half-crystal faceted beads, conterie
Marked: Made in Italy by Coppola e Toppo

Dress made for Biki, c.1960
Weft-mounted half-crystal faceted
beads in graduating tones from
black to transparent
Coppola e Toppo created a similar
outfit for Catherine Spaak for the
film *Adulterio all'italiana*, 1966

Biki sketch of the crystal bead dress

Coppola e Toppo bolero-jewel for Biki, 1965
Weft-mounted half-crystal faceted beads
Published in *Linea*, winter 1965, p.50

Biki drawing of glass pearl waistcoat for an evening dress, c.1965

Formula giovane
della sottana
di shantung-mikado
color ciclamino
(lunghezza alla caviglia,
gran nodo al centro)
per sdrammatizzare
il tutto nero
e il peso
del bolero
incrostato di jais.

BIKI

CON GIUSTO
EQUILIBRIO

Pochette and umbrella with handle covered with
weft-mounted half-crystal faceted beaded
sheath, c.1955

Cigarette box, c.1955
Metal box with pavé-embroidered half-
crystal faceted beads cover, conterie

Brooch with leaf-shaped pendant, c.1950
String-mounted half-crystal beads and pink
opaline glass spheres, conterie

"WHEN THE OUTFIT IS MADE WITH A PRINTED FABRIC, YOU NEED A JEWEL TO GO PERFECTLY WITH THE COLOUR
OR COLOURS OF THE FABRIC. OTHERWISE IT'S BETTER NOT TO WEAR ANYTHING."

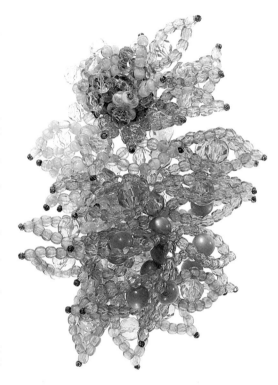

The American fashion market was hailing Coppola e Toppo fashion jewellery with the same excitement that was being seen in France. Success was marked in 1949 by a full-page colour spread that appeared in American *Vogue*,[12] showing Lyda Toppo fashion jewellery on busts of Florentine noblewomen portrayed by Antonio del Pollaiolo. There then followed countless editorial pieces in *Women's Wear Daily* and weekly magazines linked to the various American cities' most important dailies, that invariably – at least twice a year – reported on the latest novelties from the Coppola e Toppo collections.

The date of the *Vogue* editorial is particularly interesting because it bears witness to how Coppola e Toppo jewellery was amongst the first 'Made in Italy' products exported to the United States, notwithstanding the high customs duty enforced by the local government immediately after the war on luxury goods coming from overseas.

At that time in the USA there were five big names from Italian fashion that were known and admired: Ferragamo, Emilio Pucci, Roberta di Camerino (Giuliana Coen Camerino), Simonetta and the Sorelle Fontana. Ferragamo was the legendary manufacturer of elegant shoes, strictly made-to-measure, who became famous in Hollywood starting at the beginning of 1920s and in 1947 received the Neiman Marcus Fashion Award, the equivalent of an Oscar in the fashion industry. Emilio Pucci had already been the subject of a couple of pages in *Harper's Bazaar* in December 1947, when he was photographed in St. Moritz while creating a small wardrobe of ski wear for a friend who had lost her suitcase. The magazine described Pucci as one of the most imaginative and talented designers on the international fashion scene. He went on to receive the Neiman Marcus Fashion Award in 1954 and again in 1967. Roberta di Camerino, with her bags in hand-woven silk velvet, became famous in America in the immediate post-war period and in 1956 received the Neiman Marcus Fashion Award.

British *Vogue* in 1948 had dedicated a detailed feature on the austere style of Simonetta (Simonetta Colonna Cesarò) set in Capri. In January 1949, the Fontana sisters (Zoe, Micol, and Giovanna) had created the wedding dress for Linda Christian, who – much to the joy of Italian and American housewives – achieved her dream and became the wife of Tyrone Power, one of the best-loved Hollywood celebrities, in Rome, a city that was becoming the adopted home of many international movie stars at the time.

[12] American *Vogue*, 1 November 1949, p.104

Rigid necklace for Elsa Schiaparelli, first half of the 1950s
Pavé embroidered half-crystal faceted beads, conterie
Marked: Made in Italy by Coppola e Toppo

American *Vogue*, 1 November 1949, p.104
Paola Bay Archives, Milan

Festoon necklace, 1949
String-mounted glass paste spheres simulating turquoise and pavé-embroidered coral branches on horseshoe-formed metal plate
Marked: Made Italy Miky

"WHEN THE OUTFIT IS SIMPLE OR PLAIN-COLOURED, YOU CAN WEAR A FEW MORE ACCESSORIES:
NECKLACE, EARRINGS, BRACELET; BUT WATCH OUT FOR THE COLOUR MATCHING."

Giovanni Battista Giorgini (1899-1971), an enterprising
and creative Florentine nobleman, operating as a resi-
dent buyer in Florence, specialised in sourcing handcrafted Italian products suitable for export and in
particular for the American department stores. In 1948
he began to develop a strategy to launch 'Made in
Italy' fashion on the American market, non-existent
until then, because in Italy and in the world in general
it was Paris dictating the rules of fashion and
conquering foreign markets.

In February 1951, Giorgini organised the first Italian
fashion shows at his Renaissance villa in Via dei Serragli
and in the most captivating sites in artistic Florence.
Several emerging couturiers took part (Schuberth,
the Sorelle Fontana, Carosa, Maria Antonelli, Alberto
Fabiani, Simonetta, all based in Rome; Germana
Marucelli, Jole Veneziani, Noberasco and Vanna, from
Milan) and several 'boutique' (ready-to-wear)
designers: La Tessitrice dell'Isola, Bertoli, Avolio, Mirsa,
Emilio Pucci. These shows were far more successful
than anyone had expected. Giorgini, in fact, had
managed to imbue foreign buyers and journalists with
the conviction that had sustained him since the
beginning of his project, that 'Made in Italy' fashion –
colourful, imaginative, unexpected, sophisticated – was
the outcome of the legacy and tradition of the Italian
artistic heritage, with no equal anywhere in the world.
Until 1965, the fashion shows were repeated twice
a year under his direction, and until 1982, under the
supervision of others. Giorgini's plan of attracting the

Portrait of Countess Attolico di Adelfia wearing
a Coppola e Toppo simulated pearl necklace
Published in American *Vogue*, 15 March 1953, p.84

attention of some of the most important American
buyers and journalists on Italian fashion had become
a reality. And thus, after a long and laborious process
of evolution which had its roots buried deep in the
Renaissance culture, Italian fashion began to impose
itself on the international scene. The same was also
true of fashion jewellery (by Coppola e Toppo, but also
Giuliano Fratti and Luciana de Reutern) and accessories
(Canessa, Gallia & Peter, Biancalani) complementing
the dresses shown at fashion shows. Jewellery and
accessories enjoyed their moment of glory, which
lasted until the end of the 1960s.

The success of 'Made in Italy' fashion became
official in 1952 with the transfer of the fashion shows
to the *Sala Bianca*, (White Room – its name deriving
from the colour of the stucco-work framing large
mirrors) at the Palazzo Pitti. On that occasion, a journalist writing for *Novità* described the two Coppola e
Toppo pearl necklaces shown in the picture on the left
with these words: "The new interpretations of the
pearl necklace are well suited to brightening up the
slightly austere elegance of the black dress; on the left,
multiple strands are held by half-crystal clasps and on
the right, two strands of pearls end with a cluster of
pearl drops."[13]

The success of Coppola e Toppo fashion jewellery
in Italy and the legitimisation of costume jewellery as
a fashion complement, no less appropriate than fine
jewellery, was sanctioned by American *Vogue*[14] in
March 1953 which published a portrait of the Countess

[13] Vera (Vera Vaerini), 'La studiata naturalezza' in *Novità*,
19 May 1952, p.24
[14] 'Four Elegants' in American *Vogue*, 15 March 1953, p.84

Attolico di Adelfia in an evening corset dress complemented with a Coppola e Toppo pearl necklace with a rigid centre in embroidered smoke-grey crystal beads.

There are many reasons why Italian fashion became increasingly established with foreign customers in the course of the 1950s. The first reason relates to the type of dress that was being manufactured in Italy. In fact, casual but elegant boutique clothes were being proposed, together with haute couture outfits, that fully met the concept of functionality and easiness, so dear to American women, whose dresses were comfortable and easy to wear. Italian dresses had colours which referred to sea and sunny landscapes, impeccable styling, and came with shoes, belts and hats, totally handmade according to traditional handcrafted methods. Their makers either came from Roman and Florentine high society – the Marquess Emilio Pucci, the Baroness Clarette Gallotti (Tessitrice dell'Isola), the Marchioness Olga di Gresy (Mirsa), Princess Giovanna Caracciolo Ginetti (Carosa), Simonetta Colonna Cesarò married to Visconti (Simonetta) – or from the industrial bourgeoisie in the North – Elvira Leonardi Bouyeure (Biki), Giuliana Coen Camerino (Roberta di Camerino). These operators, cultivated and cosmopolitan, knew the expectations of potential foreign customers. In Italy the prices of articles produced for export were much lower than those produced in France, our formidable competitor, because here the cost of labour was lower compared to the rest of Europe. In fact, a great number

of working people needed and wanted to re-establish a normal life after the forced unemployment experienced during the war. France, moreover, was struck by a series of calamities in the course of the 1950s that weakened its leadership on the fashion scene. Several *couturiers* passed away (Jeanne Lanvin in 1946, Jacques Fath in 1954, Christian Dior in 1957) or retired (Marcelle Dormoy in 1950, Worth-Paquin and Piguet in 1953, Carpentier in 1957). Italian fashion was further helped by a series of promotional events held abroad. The costs of these events were often borne by the textile manufacturers based in northern Italy who had done so much in that decade to modernise and re-launch their sector. At other times these promotions were paid for by the organisations that had arisen immediately after the war and in the early 1950s in support of Italian fashion: in Milan (*Centro Italiano per la Moda,* 1948), in Venice (*Centro Internazionale delle Arti e del Costume,* 1951), in Rome (*Società Italiana Alta Moda,* 1954 and *Camera Nazionale d'Alta Moda Italiana,* 1962), in Florence (*Centro di Firenze per la Moda Italiana,* 1954).

Press coverage of these praiseworthy initiatives was ensured by the fashion magazines of the time, and in particular *La donna, Bellezza, Linea, Grazia* and *Novità.* Thus, as had happened in North America in the 1930s, the illustrated magazines brought fashion into Italian homes, even in areas that were quite far from the major cities. Women were helped in choosing how to dress and how to behave appropriately for the new social occasions. The rapid social and economic

changes which had taken place in Italy in just a few years, had resulted, in fact, in upgrading women's position on the social ladder. 'Made in Italy' fashion, however, was still not being conceived for the local market, where it did not represent a reality but an escape from real life. Italians were striving to imitate the life style of North America, which the allies, while liberating Italy from fascism, had personified. In political terms, Italy was looking to the United States as a privileged partner because of the American population's tendency towards consumerism, and this was seen as a way forward for the reconstruction of Italy.

The American model was also made desirable by Hollywood movies, which showed a wealthy, free, nonconformist society, where the self-made man often transformed the American dream into reality. Legendary Hollywood film stars and members of the international jet set were coming to Rome from all over the world to be dressed with 'Made in Italy' clothes and became travelling shop windows for the dressmakers who had created them. High society and fashion were becoming increasingly linked. Tourist sites for the elite – the art cities of Florence, Rome, Venice and trendy resorts such as Portofino, Positano, and Capri referred to by Italian designers through their products in Mediterranean colours – represented another major attraction of Italy in the eyes of foreigners. And so, on the one hand Italian fashion was conquering America and on the other hand, American culture was strongly influencing the Italian way of life

Necklace with cascade motif dropping from a rigid bridge-shaped element, 1954
String-mounted half-crystal beads and pavé-embroidered on central element and on the clasp, conterie
Marked: Made in Italy by Coppola e Toppo
Published in *Harper's Bazaar*, England, November 1954, p.62

– for so many years closed to the stimuli and innovations coming from other countries – where thanks to the beat of rock'n'roll, everyone dreamt of being American.

The crossover between the two cultures is documented by several fashion editorials: Irene Brin, the untiring ambassador of Italian fashion, published an article in *Bellezza* in February 1952 with the title 'Sole d'Italia in pieno inverno a New York' ('Italian sunshine in the New York winter'), in which she presented a series of sun dresses by Simonetta Visconti, "the glamorous countess"; in 1955 a report on American fashion, 'A passeggio per New York' ('Walking in New York'), appeared in *Grazia*, a magazine from Milan for middle-class readers, presenting New York's ready-to-wear dresses suitable for different circumstances and occasions for the dynamic working woman always on the go; and in the autumn of 1956 the designers Charles James (Britain), Valentina, Oleg Cassini and Pauline Trigère (USA) accepted an invitation from the *Centro Internazionale delle Arti e del Costume* in Venice and paraded eighty outfits "showing off their splendour, intelligence, organisation".[15] But Italian fashion was no less organised, as Irene Brin explained: "The expansion of Italian fashion in the 1950s and its definitive success on the international *couture* scene is not simply about the export of a style, of a material culture, but the expression of a multitude of craftsmen's sensitivities and knowledge capable of creating dresses and complements fulfilling the specific needs of other countries' women, from New York to Caracas."[16]

Until the mid-1950s, Italian fashion houses produced and showed their new collections first to American buyers and then to the buyers from other countries; France included. Bruno Coppola confirmed to me that it was the same for each new Coppola e Toppo jewellery collection, which would initially be shown to the American buyers, then to customers in France and, finally, in Italy. Impoverished by the war, as was the rest of Europe, Italy was not yet a viable market. For Coppola e Toppo, the fact of having various French couturiers as clients, served as a credential with the American buyers – the agents of one of the few markets that was able to absorb luxury goods – enchanted as always by anything that, in terms of fashion, luxury and elegance came from or was being sold in France. Using her in-depth knowledge of the international market, for many years Lyda Toppo created ornaments with the American public in mind, interpreting the expectations of this young population that was inclined towards disposable consumerism rather than bound to the tradition of family jewels.[17]

It is hardly surprising then that the American market was lauding the Coppola e Toppo creations in editorials published in their most important fashion magazines, which were then picked up by the European associate publications such as the British *Harper's Bazaar*, which in November 1954 wrote: "Many of the necklaces we love best come from Italy (hunt them out in London stores): ...Shown on these two pages, the shaded, graduated crystal of Coppola e Toppo cascading from the throat".[18]

And so the fame of Coppola e Toppo began to extend throughout the English-speaking world, even to Australia. In that same year, a page in French *Vogue* showed two Coppola e Toppo necklaces in half-crystal beads made for Christian Dior.[19]

In the Coppola e Toppo archives some letters from 1956 bear witness to the association established by Lyda Toppo with Emilio Pucci, which was to last many years. In one of these letters, the marquess, already famous in the United States, provides Lyda Toppo with the samples of printed fabrics for his forthcoming 'Siena' collection (1957).[20] Lyda develops proposals for fashion jewels attuned to the prints, that take their names from the *Contradas* of Siena rendered famous by the *Palio* – *Onda, Nicchio, Pantera, Oca, Civetta, Chiocciola, Istrice, Montone, Giraffa, Bruco, Tartuca, Aquila*. The results are colourful jewels, consisting of a rigid structure or made with string-mounted beads which complete the captivating impact of unmistakable Emilio Pucci fabric patterns with their graduated colour tones. It is this very designer, the flag-bearer of Italian beauty and fantasy who becomes Coppola e Toppo's best customer, second only to the great American luxury department stores.

From 1962, Lyda began making belts for Emilio Pucci. The belts were made with the same fabric used for the outfit, generally silk organzine cut on the bias

[15] Brin I., 'Incontro internazionale della moda a Venezia' in *Bellezza*, no. 10, 1956, pp.92-100
[16] Brin I., 'Moda italiana giramondo' in *Bellezza*, no. 4, 1956, p.124
[17] Similar to the situation in France during the post-war period, buyers in the USA or the Italian couture houses could negotiate exclusivity for certain colourways, but could never obtain exclusivity for a particular model, the ownership of which remained firmly with Coppola e Toppo. This is clear from what appeared in the fashion magazines at the time. On 1 August 1952, *Women Wear Daily* published two Coppola e Toppo necklaces, which would later appear at the Florence autumn/winter 1952/1953 fashion shows. Both were two-strand necklaces, the first with a rigid central bar embroidered with half-crystal beads and the other with a central crossed leaf motif. The first necklace appeared again a year later photographed by Elsa Robiola on a Germana Marucelli outfit in *Bellezza* (April 1953, p.70) with the following comment: "Amongst the fashion jewels, the necklaces presented by Coppola e Toppo with Marucelli outfits attracted attention in Florence for their priceless originality in terms of form, hues, materials. Here is a double loop of russet crystals fixed by a rigid bar of azure, pink and grey crystals. A square necklace effect." The second necklace was photographed in 2001 on Marisa Berenson who describes it as one of her "favourite Schiaparelli fashion jewels from amongst those inherited from Grandma Elsa".
[18] 'The bead craze' in *Harper's Bazaar*, England, November 1954, pp.62 and 63
[19] French *Vogue*, October 1954, p.100
[20] This collection was revisited in June 2007 in a beautiful exhibition staged at the museum complex of Santa Maria della Scala in Siena.

Five-strand necklace, c. 1958
String mounted glass paste spheres, oblong stones, and half-crystal faceted beads, pavé-embroidered heart-shaped clasp
Marked: Made in Italy by Coppola e Toppo
Published in *Linea*, winter 1958, p. 71, on a Biki dress

Sautoir necklace made for Christian Dior, 1954
Half-crystal faceted beads mounted to form
graduated tassels branching out from the supporting
strand, also in half-crystal faceted beads
Published in different colours in French *Vogue*,
October 1954, p. 100

and rolled up to form a tubular shape, on the ends of
which were sewn segments of string-mounted graduated half-crystal beads in colours compatible with the
fabric of the dress.

For the full necklines on the back of the early 1950s,
Lyda invented central decorative motifs that adorned
both the décolleté and the back.

In the course of that decade, the fashions began to
change and Lyda adapted by passing from collar necklaces with rigid motifs suitable for evening wear with
deep necklines to totally loose necklaces of varying
lengths, to be worn with day-wear clothes.

Beginning in 1959, the year Bruno Coppola first
travelled to the United States, American newspapers
and fashion magazines were announcing his arrival
to present the new collections of jewellery. Lord &
Taylor, the first American customer of Coppola jewellery who started selling them in 1949 was joined by
other important clients such as Saks Fifth Avenue and
Henry Bendel in New York, Neiman Marcus in Dallas,
and Henry Morgan in Canada. At the end of the 1950s,
Coppola e Toppo also became increasingly successful
in Italy. Their jewellery, photographed in the fashion
magazines of the time, show a major evolution in
design. From rigid or partially rigid necklaces, the 1960s
brought loose and soft motifs. These were made with
pierced beads strung one after the other or weft-
mounted, a method in which four beads are joined
together to form a square, which repeated many times
gives origin to a fabric made of stones. The use of this

Collar necklace, 1954
Faceted crystal beads strung and
weft-mounted on a memory wire
Published in *Harper's Bazaar*, England,
November 1954, p.63

Scarf-necklace, 1954
Half-crystal faceted beads strung to form graduated
festoons branching out from a supporting strand,
also in half-crystal faceted beads
Published in *Harper's Bazaar*, England,
November 1954, p.63

particular technique allows for the creation of motifs
(spheres, leaves, flowers), which, once attached on to
a weft-mounted base, become three-dimensional and
moving shapes.

This innovation was immediately well received. In
1959 Coppola e Toppo were supplying jewellery to two
of the most talented Italian couturiers in Florence:
Roberto Capucci (spring/summer and autumn/winter
collections 1959-1960) and Carosa (autumn/winter
collection 1959-1960). The colours of these jewels went
with the classic hues of the fabrics used for these
outfits: grey, black, particular shades of green, bright
pink, sky-blue/green and amethyst.

Four-strand collar necklace with square
centre also functioning as a clasp, 1957
Opaline glass-paste spheres strung and pavé-
embroidered on the central motif mixed with
pastel-coloured glass-paste spheres, conterie
Marked: Made in Italy by Coppola e Toppo
The same model, but in pink, was published
in *Linea Italiana*, winter 1957, p.63

Four-strand necklace, c.1954
String-mounted simulated pearls and half-crystal faceted
beads and pavé-embroidered on the square clasp
Marked: Made in Italy by Coppola e Toppo

Five-strand collar necklace, c.1954
Half-crystal faceted beads in shaded tones
from light brown to dark brown, the latter
also pavé-embroidered on a rectangular clasp
Marked: Made in Italy by Coppola e Toppo

Collar necklace, second half of 1950s
Pink glass paste spheres with beige inclusions
mounted on a weft of yellow half-crystal faceted
beads forming the outer strands and yellow with
gold-leaf inclusions forming the inner strands,
pavé-embroidery on the heart-shaped clasp
Marked: Made in Italy by Coppola e Toppo

Three-strand necklace, c. 1954
String-mounted crystal faceted beads in the rear,
weft-mounted to form leaf motifs in the front
and pavé-embroidered on the heart-shaped clasp
Marked: Made in Italy by Coppola e Toppo
Published in *Cinemoda*, special issue of
Ricostruzione Italiana, August 1954,
on Carlo De Gaspari Frezza outfit,
unnumbered advertising page

Nine-strand necklace transformable into
two bracelets, perhaps for Emilio Pucci, 1955
String-mounted half-crystal faceted beads
and pavé-embroidered on the circular clasps
Double clasp on the front and back
Published in *Women's Wear Daily*, 27 January 1956

Nine-strand necklace transformable into two
bracelets and two-strand bracelet, perhaps for
Emilio Pucci, 1955
The two-strand bracelet can substitute one of the
two nine-strand bracelets rendering the necklace less
heavy and formal. String-mounted half crystal faceted
beads in pink and violet tones and pavé-embroidered
on the double clasp, on the front and back
Published in *Women's Wear Daily*, 27 January 1956

Drawing of Emilio Pucci of the necklace
shown on the side, Florence c.1955
Tissue paper and blue and red pen

**Rigid necklace with central bracket
motif for Emilio Pucci, c.1955**
Pavé-embroidered half-crystal faceted
beads on the back part and mounted in
a 'tuft' style on the central motif
Marked: Made in Italy by Coppola e Toppo
Leila Marzagao Collection, London

Four-strand necklace with rigid motif, c.1956
String-mounted and pavé-embroidered half-crystal
faceted beads
Marked: Made in Italy
Published in *Linea Italiana*, winter 1957, p.65
and in *Le dictionnaire international du bijou*,
Editions du Regard, Paris, 1998, p.147

Festoon necklace, perhaps for Emilio Pucci, c.1955
Weft-mounted half-crystal faceted beads forming a flame design
Carolle Thibaut Pomerantz Collection, Paris

Sautoir also usable as a two-strand necklace, first half of the 1950s
Weft-mounted half-crystal faceted beads and simulated baroque pearls
Marked on clasp: Coppola Toppo

Lyda Coppola wearing the necklace
shown left, c.1955
A necklace, similar to the one shown
opposite (but made of spheres of glass
paste simulating hard stones, c.1955) is
displayed on the stand in the foreground
Ginger Moro Archives, Los Angeles

Large seven-strand necklace with
memory-wire collar, 1958
String and weft-mounted half-crystal
faceted beads forming a sheath containing
a memory wire
Published in *Women's Wear Daily*,
20 August 1958

Demi-parure made up of four-strand necklace
with rigid double-loop central motif and
earrings, perhaps for Emilio Pucci, c.1957
String mounted and pavé-embroidered half-
crystal faceted beads and central motif
Marked: Made in Italy by Coppola e Toppo
Paola Bay Collection, Milan

Five-strand necklace, c.1958
String-mounted glass paste spheres and half-crystal faceted
beads, pavé-embroidered on the heart-shaped clasp
Marked: Made in Italy by Coppola e Toppo

Five-strand necklace, second half of the 1950s
String-mounted half-crystal faceted beads and
metallic red-painted glass spheres
Marked on one clasp bar: Made in Italy
Marked on the other clasp bar: by Coppola e Toppo

Demi-parure made up of necklace and bracelet, c. 1958
String-mounted necklace in graduated lustred half-crystal
faceted beads branching off a sheath also made of weft-
mounted half-crystal beads covering a memory wire
Bracelet made with weft-mounted crystals forming a
sheath containing a memory wire and two wooden spheres

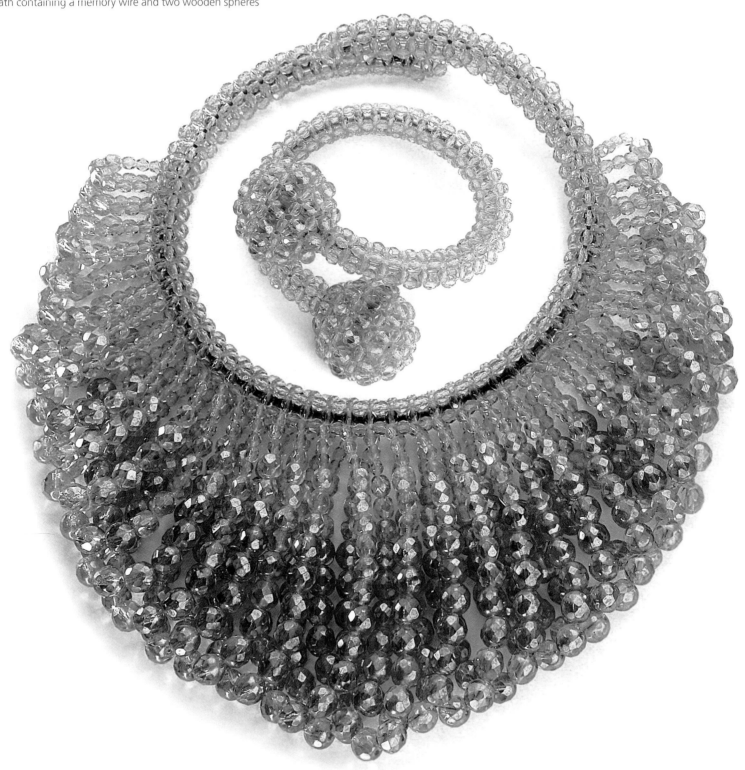

Necklace with side leaf motifs, 1958
String-mounted half-crystal faceted beads forming leaf
motifs and pavé-embroidered on the heart-shaped clasp
Marked: Made in Italy by Coppola e Toppo
Published in black and white in *Linea*, spring 1958, p.88
Leila Marzagao Collection, London

Seven-strand necklace with side bow motif, 1959
String-mounted half-crystal faceted beads and
weft-mounted for the bow part
Marked: Made in Italy by Coppola e Toppo
Published in *Chicago Daily Tribune*, 13 October 1959
Leila Marzagao Collection, London

Festoon necklace, second half of the 1950s
Glass-faceted cones strung with conterie to form
petals attached to weft of glass beads underneath
Marked: Made in Italy by Coppola e Toppo

Nine-strand collar necklace, 1959
String-mounted half-crystal faceted beads
and pavé-embroidered on heart-shaped clasp
The same model in different colours was
published in *Linea*, spring 1959, p.70
Mania Hruska Collection, Milan

Eight-strand necklace, perhaps for Emilio Pucci, c.1959
String-mounted half-crystal faceted beads and pavé-
embroidered on the heart-shaped clasp
Marked: Made in Italy by Coppola e Toppo

Belt for an Emilio Pucci outfit made by Coppola e Toppo, c.1962
String-mounted graduated half-crystal faceted beads hanging
from organzine silk sheath

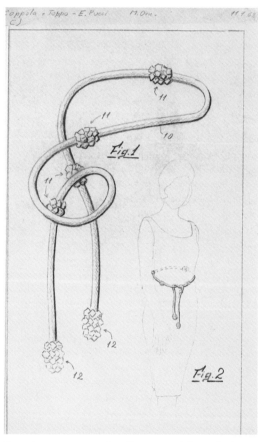

Drawing accompanying the request for a design
patent of a belt presented by Coppola e Toppo
and Emilio Pucci, Rome, 1962

Leaf-shaped collar necklace, 1959
Weft-mounted half-crystal faceted beads forming leaf
motifs and pavé-embroidered on heart-shaped clasp, 1959
Marked: Made in Italy by Coppola e Toppo
Published in *Women's Wear Daily*, 19 June 1959

Three-strand necklace with central ball
motifs, perhaps for Roberto Capucci, 1959
Weft and string-mounted half-crystal
faceted beads forming ball motifs and
pavé-embroidered on heart-shaped clasp
Marked: Coppola Toppo

Choker, c. 1959
String-mounted half-crystal faceted beads
and fixed on underlying weft with leaf-shaped
decorative elements made with silver plated
wire, *roses montées* and glass spheres
Marked: Made in Italy by Coppola e Toppo
Marina Gregotti Collection, Milan

105

Festoon necklace, 1959
Black and transparent half-crystal faceted beads
strung to form graduated tassels mounted on
underlying weft in transparent half crystals beads,
pavé-embroidered heart-shaped clasp
Marked: Coppola Toppo
Published in *Women's Wear Daily*, 13 October 1959

Collar necklace with leaf motif, late 1950s
Grey and white simulated pearls strung to form leaf motifs
Donatella Pellini Collection, Milan

THE SECRET TO SUCCESS

"REMEMBER THAT A PIECE OF COSTUME JEWELLERY WILL NEVER BE AN ORNAMENT TO GO WITH EVERYTHING. IT WILL BE PERFECT FOR A PARTICULAR OUTFIT, OR AT BEST, FOR A GROUP OF OUTFITS."

Coppola e Toppo clients included the great and the beautiful, as Lyda explained: "Amongst those best known to the public, Princess Lee Radziwill, Audrey Hepburn, Jackie Kennedy Onassis, Lady Astor, Princess Alessandra Lequio Torlonia and many others. But when they come to me, even if I recognise them, I address all of them with a simple *signora* because I imagine that they too, all told, don't like to be recognised. I don't like being pushy, it would seem as if I was forcing them to identify themselves. Choosing a piece of jewellery should be like a holiday, a light-hearted break."[21] That so many famous and important women should choose to wear Lyda's creations can surely be seen as a great triumph. So, to what did she owe her great success?

The answer can be summed up in just a few simple words: the right product at the right time. The high craftsmanship represented by the embroidery of beads, Lyda Toppo's speciality, found its market in countries that looked to Italy as the land of art and beauty. Fashion jewellery is, moreover, an element that distinguishes and personalises an outfit, an important feature at the time of the start-up of the company, whose activity grew hand-in-hand with the success of ready-made outfits, especially in North America.

But, of course, there are many reasons for the success of Coppola e Toppo production, particularly their fashion jewellery, but also the scarves, bags, umbrella handles covered with weft-mounted half-crystal beads, boxes with stone-embroidered lids, and dress trimmings.

Lyda's creativity, based on her knowledge of history of art; her great sensitivity for colours; her technical experience; the ability of the craftsmen and of her specialist women workers; the professionalism of her brother Bruno, a tireless businessman and great communicator, capable of winning the favour and cultivating the loyalty from every kind of buyer – all of these elements together help to explain the company's success and the growth rate of sales of Coppola e Toppo creations, despite their fairly high cost. Lyda's creativity stands out in Coppola e Toppo models, obtained through painstaking manual work applied to a vast range of materials, especially vitreous, extremely varied, and sometimes used for the first time in the creation of non-precious ornaments. The different materials were assembled one with the other in different hues and measures, so as to obtain cascades of colours in the most stunning shades that one could imagine, harmoniously paired or deliberately contrasting. In the immediate post-war period, Lyda Coppola's choice of materials fell on pure crystal beads, coral, malachite, garnet, turquoise, jade, chalcedony, and on glass paste simulating those semi-precious stones, string-mounted and finished with a strictly handmade brass clasp, sometimes decorated by cameos. In 1950, Lyda Coppola began using pure crystal faceted beads – which had a high shine due to the high content of lead – paired with other half-crystal beads – less sparkling because of the lower lead content – both manufactured in Bohemia and often mentioned as 'jais' by the journalists of the time.

Perhaps it was because of the high cost of pure crystal that Lyda soon decided to opt for the half-crystal faceted beads, the material that became the company's emblem, with a choice of one hundred and forty different shades. To the beads we must add the small Venetian *conterie* (small pierced glass beads) in multiple colours, used to fill in the small gaps left between one bead and the next. If I wanted to describe a colour from the countless shades used in Coppola e Toppo jewellery, for example azure/ turquoise, I think back to the words said by Emilio Pucci to Nanda Calandri when describing his "water" hues: "I discovered them while diving. I couldn't find a turquoise as beautiful as the one on hand-painted Mexican fabrics; I took about five hundred photographs underwater, near Marina Piccola in Capri, where the rocks are submerged about thirty metres in water that changes colour: white, pale green, palest blue, pale turquoise, ocean green, sapphire, the colour of the *Grotta Azzurra* (Blue Grotto). That's how my 'water' colours were born".[22]

[21] Fogliani P., *ibid*
[22] Calandri N., *Storie e favole di moda*, Florence, 1982

Snake bracelet, c.1950
String-mounted simulated pearls and
pavé-embroidered pure crystal faceted
beads mounted on central motif and clasp
Marked on clasp: Made in Italy
Marked on rigid elements: Made Italy

The words of Pucci could easily describe one of the many azure necklaces by Lyda Coppola, cascading from the throat rather than embroidered: a piece of the sea stolen from nature to be hung around the neck of a woman!

Pierced beads, from the tiny *conterie* to the faceted half-crystal beads and glass paste spheres, were purchased by Coppola e Toppo in all carats, including the half-millimetre measurement, from three millimetres in diameter to fourteen, without exception. However, the stones used by Coppola e Toppo were not just simple coloured crystal beads but were additionally treated with processes that were superimposed on the initial colour such as: lustring, an effect similar to oxidation; lustre-colouring, a high-temperature ancient glass decorative method; and high vacuum metal deposition rendering the beads iridescent. The characteristics given by the treatments of the stone colours increased the beauty of the half-crystal beads and, at the same time, differentiated Coppola e Toppo raw materials from those used by other fashion jewellers.

Together with half-crystal faceted beads – the material most often used – other glass stones were employed to simulate semiprecious stones, and these too were in a multitude of shades, from the bright green of malachite to the blue ash grey of chalcedony. In the jewels created by Lyda Coppola, though, the most important element was not the material, but the way it was used: "The idea is nothing – she once said – ideas come to me by the dozen. The difficult thing is giving a form to them. ...In fact, it's always about resolving a different problem, adapting, case by case, the materials to the model, and the technical process to the materials, even inventing new techniques, trying them and then retrying them, remaking the first specimen up to twenty to thirty times, and dedicating from four to fourteen hours of work on the subsequent specimens".[23]

An article dedicated to the production of post-war fashion jewellery commented: "To limit ourselves to the fashion jewellery field, we must disclose here how the input of Italian creativity, especially that of Mrs. Coppola-Toppo, has been important and unique considering her breaking away from working with rhinestones, a typically French technique in origin that has long reigned over the past years. To counter rhinestones, she uses crystal beads, pearls and coral, whose colours, faceted features and the variety of forms have allowed for wider and bolder combinations of materials and hues. The incomparable artistic heritage of Italy provided Lyda with the greatest starting points in the creation of necklaces, bracelets, brooches and earrings. Her imagination allowed her to run wild, from season to season, in the choice of a theme or a dominant colour thus proving that fashion and art were closely connected. Nevertheless, what characterises Coppola e Toppo production is the fact that it does not imitate fine jewels – since crystal beads, coral and pearls are used and exploited for their peculiar characteristics – thus deserving the definition of *bijoux de voyage* (travel jewels) given to them by Madame Schiaparelli."[24]

Until the second half of the 1950s, some pieces of Coppola e Toppo jewellery consisted partially (until 1950) or entirely (after 1950) of beads embroidered on rigid elements. These were made from a support in metal plate, generally brass, that, having a smooth and polished surface, ensured that the piece of jewellery could be worn on bare skin. The edges of these support plates were equipped with prongs that, once bent, would hold in place a metal plate with holes (beading screen) of the same shape entirely embroidered with stones. The same cord, be it copper, silk or nylon, was passed through a pierced bead and each bead was positioned next to another. The cord was then passed through one of the beading screen holes and made to come out of the next hole, ready to be threaded through the next bead and so on and so forth to cover the metal structure entirely with stones. As the cord passed through the holes in the stones and the holes in the beading screen, it was then tightened to avoid any

[23] Ravaioli C., 'L'arte del gioiello finto' in *Successo*, June 1967, p.140
[24] 'Bijoux de voyage' in *Commercio estero*, July-August 1953, p.20

Demi-parure made up of sautoir and dangling
earrings for Emilio Pucci, c.1960
Half-crystal faceted beads strung to form a leaf motif
starting from a central strand
Marked on earrings: Made in Italy by Coppola e Toppo
A variation with small gilded balls inside the leaf was
published in French *Vogue*, August 1960, p.108, while
a further model in pink hues for Emilio Pucci appeared
on the cover of *Novità*, May 1964

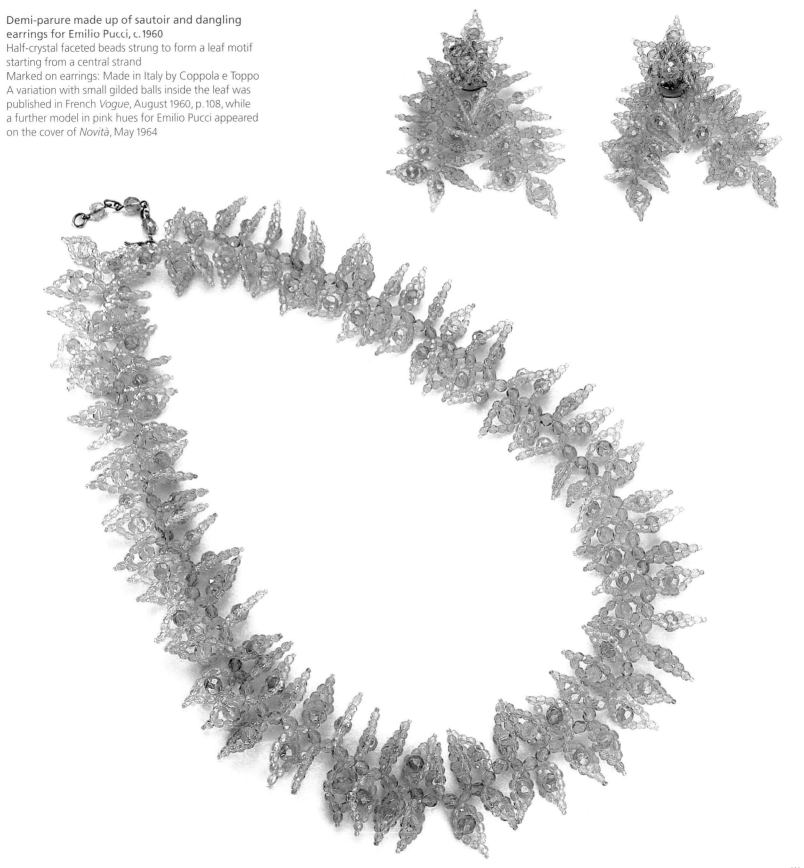

possible movement. The beading screen was not just used to set the stones in the desired position, but also to guarantee the right consistency of the embroidery. The metal supports with their ornamental function and the corresponding beading screen were always designed by Lyda and exclusively handmade for Coppola e Toppo by skilled local craftsmen.

There were two types of embroidery: one pavé-style, where the beads or spheres were placed one next to the other on the beading screen, refinished with small glass conterie in an identical or contrasting colour to cover the small gaps that remained between the stones. The other type of embroidery was, instead, the "tuft" style. With this term we mean an ornament made up of elements of varying lengths, protruding (tuft) or cascading (tassel) from a rigid structure. The segments here were made in graduated-size beads, from the smallest to the largest, and then mounted on the beading screen one next to the other in such a way as to not leave any empty spaces in between and create the shape of a tuft or a tassel.

After the first half of the 1950s, Coppola e Toppo jewellery was made mostly by using the manual threading technique, which does not mean the simple stringing in sequence of one bead after another. It is very difficult, in fact, to describe in words the construction technique adopted by Lyda when making

each piece of jewellery. She was personally responsible for the design and the creation of the first prototype which was then repeated by her specialist workers. We all know that stringing beads consists in pairing one stone after another and passing the cord through their holes. In the case of Coppola e Toppo jewellery, however, the strands overlap and intertwine, the round, oval and rectangular charms and pendants made with half-crystal beads, imitation pearls, rhinestones, plastic, bamboo pieces, opaque or glossy stones are developed as extensions of the supporting strand without breaking off the cord.

Another type of threading that Coppola e Toppo adopted, particularly in the 1960s, was mounting beads to obtain a weft through a method in which four beads were strung to form a square. This process would be repeated until the result was a weaved stone pattern.

Earrings, bracelets and brooches created by Lyda Coppola after the war and in the early 1950s were very decorative compositions, often designed as a single ornament for cocktail dresses and executed in one of those neutral tones that had been all the rage from 1947, the year Dior's New Look was born, until the mid-1950s. Throughout this period, Lyda Toppo was working in complete freedom, as none of the couturiers she got orders from made specific requests but chose instead from the already finished jewellery she proposed.

When, from the mid-1950s onwards, she started working with Italian designers, Lyda began taking their requests and suggestions into account, each time adapting her style to the customer's requirements.

As we have written previously, until the early 1960s, the couturiers were ordering jewellery with significant thrift and therefore the production of each model could vary from five to twenty pieces per season. Considering that the most popular models were remade over time, even for five consecutive years, we can assume that the production of each model in this time period could range from one hundred to one hundred and fifty specimens.

From the early 1960s onwards, with the designs of outfits becoming increasingly sleeker, almost geometric, fashion jewellery started becoming much larger in size and so required technical solutions aimed at reducing its weight. Thus Lyda began introducing plastic to replace glass beads where large measures would ultimately prove too heavy, mixed with brightly-coloured half-crystal beads and glass paste stones, perfectly compatible with the multicoloured printed fabrics of Pucci, Ken Scott and Galitzine. The visual effect of the outfits complemented by fashion jewellery moving around the neck, the face, on the ears, on the hair, reminds one of the colours of the deep-blue sea, burning flames, green lawns strewn

Festoon necklace, c.1958
Graduated string-mounted lustred half-crystal faceted beads branching off a weft-mounted sheath, also in half-crystal beads, mounted on a memory wire

with multicoloured flowers.

In the 1960s, with the economic boom in Italy and the affirmation of the Coppola e Toppo trademark in the United States, the production of pieces for each model began increasing, ultimately reaching about 300 specimens for necklaces and bracelets and more than 1000 for earrings; being quicker to make and therefore less expensive, these sold in bigger quantities.

It was a different story for those jewels destined for fashion shows and photo shoots. These were generally made in a very limited number, never more than three specimens.

In the course of the years, the materials adopted by Coppola e Toppo changed and evolved, particularly in 1967, with the start of a close collaboration with Valentino Garavani, known as Valentino. The half-crystal faceted beads were replaced by gilded, silver-plated aluminium cylindrical little tubes, sometime anodised, in colours ranging from azure, blue, brown, to rifle grey. The same tubes were also made of glass, black or painted by hand in varying colours. Very often the aluminium and the glass tubes were interspersed with *roses montées* (flat rhinestones mounted on a pierced metal setting, so that they can be strung). To start with the tubes were used to make abstract

shapes, but later were mounted in order to create leaf motifs. From 1967 onwards, wood and plastic elements, together with gilded, silver-plated or enamelled metal pieces were added to half-crystal beads.

Speaking of materials, Lyda Coppola said once: "It's not the material in itself, but how it's used, how it's manipulated, how it's paired that makes the difference between one fashion jeweller and another."[25]

Being handmade guarantees that every Coppola e Toppo item, even derived from the same model, is unique – bearing witness to having been made, each time, by different hands and in different times. On careful inspection, some variations, even if unremarkable, can always be found: slight changes in the colours of the stones; a different clasp from the one normally used for that model; or variation in the size of the stones. In any case, the object ready for sale is always impeccable, finished in every little detail with refined materials often made exclusively for Coppola e Toppo; ready to sit on the décolleté, or fall from the ear lobe or the wrist, with grace and elegance.

[25] Fogliani P., *ibid*

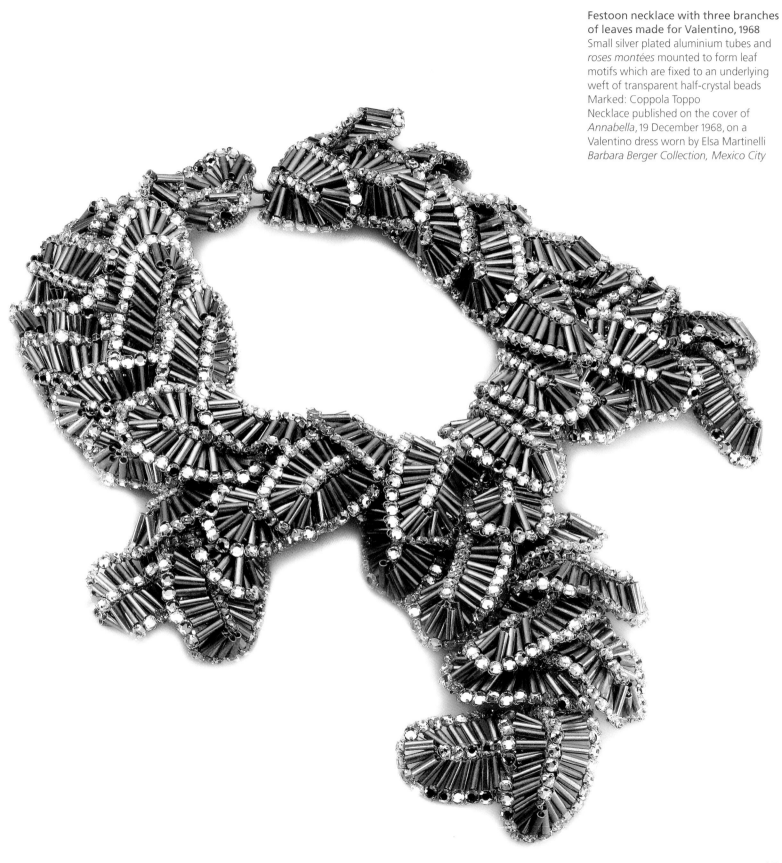

Festoon necklace with three branches
of leaves made for Valentino, 1968
Small silver plated aluminium tubes and
roses montées mounted to form leaf
motifs which are fixed to an underlying
weft of transparent half-crystal beads
Marked: Coppola Toppo
Necklace published on the cover of
Annabella, 19 December 1968, on a
Valentino dress worn by Elsa Martinelli
Barbara Berger Collection, Mexico City

Five-strand necklace with side cascading motif
String-mounted half-crystal faceted beads and
'tuft' style – embroidered on circular brass clasp
Marked: Made in Italy by Coppola e Toppo
Published in *Chicago Herald Tribune*,
13 October 1959
Leila Marzagao Collection, London

Necklace, c.1960
Weft-mounted half-crystal faceted beads
and simulated baroque pearls
Marked: Made in Italy by Coppola e Toppo

Collar necklace made for Ken Scott, 1965
Plastic faceted beads strung to form tassels
hanging from central supporting strand
Marked on the hook clasp: Coppola Toppo
Published in *Linea*, winter 1965, p.37, and in
Italian *Vogue*, February 1969, p.77

The model Marina Schiano wears the
same necklace in a different colourway
Photo shoot by Gian Paolo Barbieri for
Italian *Vogue*, September 1967, p.210

Graduated semi-sphere necklace with pendant, 1964
Weft-mounted half-crystal faceted bead base forming
semi-sphere motifs on which Swarovski "Margarita"
stones are applied
Marked: Made in Italy by Coppola e Toppo
Published in *Bellezza*, September 1964, p.27

Cluster clip, perhaps for Emilio Pucci,
second half of the 1960s
Half-crystal and plastic faceted beads fixed
to the underlying weft of half-crystal beads
Marked on brass base: Made in Italy by
Coppola e Toppo
Donatella Pellini Collection, Milan

Scallop necklace from a model of 1960, c.1965
String-mounted half-crystal faceted beads fixed
to the underlying weft of half-crystal beads
Marked: Coppola Toppo

121

Demi-parure made up of necklace and
bracelet, perhaps for Emilio Pucci, c.1965
Faceted lustred Swarovski crystal cylinders
and faceted plastic beads
Marked: Made in Italy by Coppola e Toppo

Demi-parure made up of necklace, bracelet and earring for
Gattinoni, autumn/winter collection 1969-1970
Blue-painted small glass tubes mounted together with *roses montées*
forming leaf motifs, plexiglas flowers with a rhinestone in the centre
Marked on brass clasp: Made in Italy by Coppola e Toppo
A simplified version of the same model was published in
Linea Italiana, autumn/winter 1969/70, p.120
Donatella Pellini Collection, Milan

Three-strand necklace, c.1974
Graduated plastic spheres simulating
tortoise shell, rectangular rhinestones set
and mounted to form rhinestone rondelles
Marked: Coppola Toppo
Private Collection, Milan

Mirella Petteni is wearing Coppola e Toppo
jewellery on a Valentino dress
Photograph taken by Gian Paolo Barbieri for an
advertising page that appeared in Italian *Vogue*,
March 1969

"FOR THE DAY DRESS, I ADVISE JUST SMALL EARRINGS, NOT TOO VISIBLE, OR ELSE A NECKLACE. FOR A LUNCH MEETING, EARRINGS AND A NECKLACE. FOR THE AFTERNOON, YOU CAN ADD ONE OR TWO EXTRA ITEMS, OR EVEN BETTER, SUBSTITUTE A SIMPLE JEWEL WITH A SLIGHTLY MORE IMPORTANT ONE. FOR THE EVENING, YOU CAN INCREASE THE NUMBER OF JEWELS, ESPECIALLY IN THE SUMMER. FOR A LONG EVENING GOWN, A LOT DEPENDS ON THE CUT OF THE DRESS BECAUSE THE JEWEL HAS TO HIGHLIGHT ITS STYLE. I SUGGEST LONG NECKLACES IF THE OUTFIT IS FLOWING, COLLAR NECKLACES IF THE LINE OF THE OUTFIT IS ELABORATE."

"The 1960s can be defined as the years of the democratisation of exclusive consumerism, in almost all the product sectors, from clothing to furniture, from holidays to motor vehicles."[26]

1960 saw the start of a golden decade for Italy in general and for Coppola e Toppo in particular. These were the economic boom years, marked by the widespread growth of television sets in the homes of Italians, the success of the Fiat 500, and the Vespa and Lambretta scooters.

Many movie stars – from Ingrid Bergman to Ava Gardner, from Anita Ekberg to Brigitte Bardot – appeared to be hopelessly in love with only Italian men and Rome was becoming the Hollywood of Italy where "life was sweet", as Fellini's film, *La Dolce Vita* declared, not only for tourists but also for its residents, who were *Poveri ma belli* (Poor but beautiful – another famous film). Luxury products such as tailor-made clothes or the *haute gamme* Coppola e Toppo fashion jewellery, which, just a few years earlier, had been set aside exclusively for the Roman aristocracy and foreign clients, were also becoming consumer goods for the industrial bourgeoisie, particularly in the north of Italy.

The "youth-quake" burst onto the social scene with a bang, and so many of the conventions dictated by fashion began fading into the background, the parading of wealth in the way one dressed became outmoded and many accessories such as hats and gloves, only a few years earlier considered essential for formal occasions, disappeared from women's wardrobes. At the start of the 1960s, after John Fitzgerald Kennedy had won the US presidential elections in November 1960, Pop Art made its appearance at the Venice Biennale, preceded by some happenings that mixed life and art. In these 'performances', the artist was the director and the public was the star.

The world of the couturiers and the fashion designers had to conform. The ostentation of the recent past was set aside and replaced by pure, geometric lines, with particular attention dedicated to the functionality of the short skirt and bright colours, often paired together in a non-conventional manner. Long gowns disappeared and were substituted by simple black sheath dresses with bold accessories, such as a showy brooch or an elegant necklace. (The necklace on the simple black Givenchy dress worn by Audrey Hepburn in *Breakfast at Tiffany's* springs to mind!) The Coppola e Toppo necklace (see right) made from small black glass tubes forming leaf-shaped motifs whose outlines are accentuated by *roses monteés* is an extraordinary example of a piece of costume jewellery meant to lighten the austerity of the classic little black dress.

With the end of the 1950s, when *prêt-à-porter* began to take over from high fashion in France, the request from the couturiers increasingly turned towards large-sized fashion jewellery, almost as if wanting to make up for the under-refinement of the ready-made dress. And so during the course of the 1960s, accessories began to change from simple dress complements into increasingly crucial elements in the fashion system.

The great event that left its mark on 1960 was the 'Italian Fortnights', a fifteen-day exhibition dedicated to Italian High Fashion and sponsored in Dallas by Stanley Marcus, the owner of the Neiman Marcus department-stores. This event was brilliantly described by Irene Brin in a Milan newspaper: "Mr. Stanley Marcus, Star of Italian Solidarity, is perhaps the biggest billionaire amongst the many Texan billionaires. Texas has an almost romantic sense of its wealth, deriving equally from oil and sheep farming. This is where you find the ladies that order an emerald necklace with a miniscule but complete air-conditioning facility, so that their make-up remains fresh during those brief seconds that pass from getting out of their air-conditioned cars and getting into the place they are heading for, club, home, cinema, always totally air-conditioned. This is where you find the ladies that move between their ranches and their oil wells by using one or two light aircrafts, just like 'Lady Byrd', wife of the Democrat Vice-Presidential candidate Lyndon Johnson. It's always these magnificent Texan ladies that order bedspreads in petit point from the Duke of Windsor (a fine embroiderer)...

In the presence of the Italian Ambassador, Manlio Brusio, a gigantic Italian exhibition was inaugurated in this department store. It took two years to make the preparations and two million dollars were spent in Italy.[27] During the inauguration the Ambassador

[26] Ragone G., 'I consumi in Italia fra "novità", "distinzione" e "qualità" ' in *La moda Italiana-Dall'antimoda allo stilismo*, Electa, Milan, 1987, p.10
[27] Author's note: This was funded by the Italian government

Choker made for Valentino, 1968
Small black glass tubes and *roses montées* mounted
on a weft of black half-crystal faceted beads
Marked: Made in Italy by Coppola e Toppo
Published in *Annabella*, 19 December 1968, pp.54-55
worn by Elsa Martinelli on a Valentino dress
Mania Huska Collection, Milan

stood next to Aldo Borletti and Dino Olivetti, among others; many other major trade names from Italian industry were represented by machinery or by goods of all kinds.

In the end a fast jet brought its plane-load of personalities to Dallas Airport... many famous fashion designers (Micol Fontana, Eleonora Garnett, Antonio de Luca), many important craftsmen (the Marchioness di Gresy, Fiammetta Fanti, Bruno Coppola, Lyda Toppo) and diplomats, journalists and photographers."[28]

The American and Italian newspapers gave the event a lot of coverage. The *Dallas Morning News* dated 17 October 17 1960 dedicated an entire page to the event, with engaging headlines such as "Glittering Ball" and "The best dressed". The *Corriere d'Informazione* of 1-2 November, 1960 had a full page from Irene Brin provocatively headlined: *"Rimodellata l'Italia per le donne del Texas"* ("Italy remodelled for Texan women") with the drawings of four of the models presented at the Texan exhibition: an Eleonora Garnett dress, a Fabiani mantle, another one by De Luca, and a Biki-designed evening dress with the bolero entirely made by Coppola e Toppo in half-crystal beads.

The *Dallas Morning News* from 20 October 20, 1960 again dedicated three columns on the presence of Lyda Toppo and Bruno Coppola, photographed together with Wilma Carita – one of the six models who came from Italy for the High Fashion show – wearing a necklace that is today one of the most sought-after by collectors of vintage jewellery from the many created by Lyda Toppo (see right).

Festoon necklace, 1960
Weft-mounted half-crystal faceted beads
forming an ajour (open-work) motif with
plastic faceted beads internally
Marked: Made in Italy by Coppola e Toppo
Published in *The Dallas Morning News*,
20 October 1960

The advert that appeared in the *Dallas Morning News* on 21 October, 1960 announcing the availability of the new Coppola fashion jewellery collection at the Neiman Marcus store sounds legendary. The drawing of a four-scallop necklace in two contrasting colours, that has since become a classic for collectors of vintage jewellery, comes with the following caption:

What a wizard! Italy's Madame Coppola Toppo has come for our Fortnights with her collection of the most inventive, hand-manipulated artistry in crystal. Above, the scallops of coruscating crystals is but one brilliant example. No wonder we sought her out in Italy just as we do all the best fashion houses of Europe.

In the fashion shows in Florence in January 1961, Coppola e Toppo jewellery, buttons and belts accompanied the collections of Capucci, De Luca, Carosa, de Barentzen and Aris–Lancetti, on his début at Palazzo Pitti.

The three Fontana sisters, already famous in the United States for the outfits created for many Hollywood stars passing through Rome, before presenting their 1960 winter collection in their home country, paraded their collection in New York and Washington with their outfits accompanied by Coppola e Toppo jewellery.

In 1961 Lyda Toppo formalised a contract that saw her collaborate as a designer with Geno Ltd, a fashion jewellery company with headquarters in New York, whose stylist, Norma Wessinger, began adapting the original Italian Coppola e Toppo models to suit the tastes of American women.

In an article dated July 1961 dedicated to the winter collection presented by Carosa at Palazzo Pitti with Coppola e Toppo jewellery, Luciana Olivetti Rason wrote: "All together a delightfully coquettish woman who loves all those feminine details, light and also a little vain: lace, gathered flounces, sequin-speckled tulle, a flimsy chiffon dress, a brocade mantle and everything enriched by so many beautiful necklaces – created by Coppola e Toppo – formed by cascades and intertwining strands mixing opaque stones and shiny crystals with art."[29]

It is during these years that the *bijou de couture* begins to assume such importance in fashion that a journalist is induced to write: "Because the woman is like a magpie and a newborn stretching out its little hands towards anything that shines. Perhaps it is for this reason that in the large fashion shows, the part set aside to fashion jewellery is dealt with in a special way, so much so that 'fashion' necklaces now carry a designer label just like outfits and one talks of a Dior, a Cardin, a Carousel and a Coppola e Toppo jewel with the same interest that ladies generally reserve to the dress models."[30]

1962 saw a further spreading of the fame of Coppola e Toppo. In January, in the Italian High Fashion shows in Florence, their fashion jewellery accompanied Lancetti outfits (1962-1963 spring/summer and autumn/winter collection) Carosa, Germana Marucelli, Enzo, De Luca, Patrick de Barentzen, Gianni Baldini – whose collection was designed by a young Walter Albini – and Forquet, these last two on their début

at the *Sala Bianca* at Palazzo Pitti. Speaking about jewellery, Egle Monti said: "As usual, it is Coppola e Toppo who provide the most brilliant jewels and that in this collection linger on the pearls."[31]

For the rich mantles and *tailleurs* proposed by de Barentzen, Coppola e Toppo exclusively created and produced a large button made with opaline (milk) glass spheres to be used as a single decorative element. That year, de Barentzen found a curious way to make sure he got press coverage in the fashion magazines. Anticipating the choices made by many couturiers in the 1980s, de Barentzen was the first designer in Italy to use a Eurasian model on the catwalk, Miss China Machado, Countess de la Salle, who personified his ideal of beauty and elegance. To dress Miss Machado, Patrick de Barentzen and his partner Gilles chose warm, exotic, brilliant colours, sometimes iridescent like butterfly wings, accompanied by dramatic, bold jewels by Coppola e Toppo.

De Barentzen also presented a collection of evening dresses with small boleros, again from Coppola e Toppo, made entirely of weft-mounted crystal beads that brilliantly substituted even the most magnificent jewels. In that same collection, de Barentzen launched the fashion of the single dangling earring that resembled a bunch of grapes, made with oblong glass paste stones. Egle Monti explained: "The earring is always one only and it is attached from the ear of the visible part of the face, where the hat is slightly raised, Goya-style."[32]

[28] Brin I., 'Il jet sbarca a Dallas una tarantella in costume' in *Corriere di Informazione*, 25-26 October 1960, p.3
[29] Olivetti Rason I., 'Linea Fluida o linea modellata interrogativo della stagione' in *La nazione*, 18 July 1961
[30] Monti E., 'Il gioiello decisamente falso assume spesso aspetti grotteschi' in *Il Tempo*, 16 October 1961
[31] Monti E., 'Ispirati dall'età romantica i creatori della nuova moda' in *Il Tempo*, 18 January 1962
[32] Monti E., *ibid*

Festoon necklace, c.1960
Weft-mounted simulated baroque pearls
Marked: Made in Italy by Coppola e Toppo
Private Collection, Pisa

Scallop necklace, 1960
Half-crystal faceted beads and simulated baroque pearls mounted
on a weft of half-crystal beads, pavé-embroidered brass clasp
Marked: Coppola Toppo
Published in *The Dallas Morning News*, 21 October 1960
Private Collection, Milan

Festoon necklace, c.1960
Half-crystal faceted beads mounted as a weft
from which small graduated tassels descend
Marked: Coppola Toppo

Three sautoirs, second half of the 1960s
Transparent iridescent half-crystal faceted beads
and coloured plastic beads strung to form loops
Marked on the hook clasp: Coppola

Three-strand loop necklace, c.1960
Half-crystal faceted beads strung to form loops,
pavé-embroidery on the heart-shaped clasp
Marked: Coppola Toppo

Handbag and four-strand loop necklace,
first half of the 1960s
Handbag: weft-mounted half-crystal faceted
beads with pommels covered in weft-mounted
beads. Necklace: weft-mounted half-crystal
faceted beads string-mounted to form loops,
clasp covered in pavé embroidery
Marked on the necklace: Made in Italy
by Coppola e Toppo
Maura Caminada Collection, Milan

Handbag, c.1962
Weft-mounted half-crystal faceted beads, gilded
metal handle and clasp, also in metal, partially
covered in a weft of half-crystal beads
Silk label sewn on the inside: Made in Italy
Paola Bay Collection, Milan

Ball necklace, c.1960 taken from a model of the mid-1950s
String and weft-mounted half-crystal faceted beads forming
boules containing synthetic sponge and *roses montées* strung
on silver plated wire to form leaf branches
Marked: Coppola Toppo

Loop *sautoir* **for Lancetti, 1961**
Weft-mounted black half-crystal faceted beads
Published on cover of *Rossana*, January 1962

Two-handle handbag, c.1965
Weft-mounted plastic faceted beads and plastic discs
Fabric label: Made in Italy expressly for Alexander's

Tie necklace with tartan motif, 1961
Weft-mounted half-crystal faceted beads
Marked on the necklace clasp: Made in Italy
by Coppola e Toppo

Tie necklace, 1961
String and weft-mounted half-crystal faceted
beads, with insertion of coral branches
Published in *Il Tempo*, 19 January 1962 and on
a Federico Forquet dress in *La Settimana
Radio TV*, 25 February 1962, p.49

Festoon necklace, 1961
Copper chain linking weft-mounted
strips of half-crystal faceted beads
Marked: Made in Italy by Coppola e Toppo
Published in American *Vogue*,
September 1963, p. 197

142

Tie necklace, 1961
Weft-mounted half-crystal faceted
black and steel-coloured beads
forming a diagonal motif
Marked: Coppola Toppo

Bib necklace, 1962
Graduated string-mounted half-crystal faceted beads
descending from a supporting strand and ending with
a glass pearl
Marked: Coppola Toppo

Necklace with central loops, 1961
String-mounted simulated pearls and
weft-mounted half-crystal faceted beads
Made from a drawing by Lyda Coppola
adapted by Norma Wessinger of Geno Ltd.
Published in different colours in *Women's Wear Daily*, 5 May 1961

Necklace with scallop motif, 1962
String-mounted simulated pearls and half-crystal faceted beads, the latter also weft-mounted on the rear of the necklace, pavé embroidered heart-shaped clasp
Marked. Made in Italy by Coppola e Toppo
Published in different colours in *Grazia*, 9 December 1962, p. 55
Private Collection, Pisa

Four intertwined strand necklace with ball motifs, 1962
String and weft-mounted half-crystal faceted beads forming
'boules', pavé embroidery on the heart-shaped clasp
Marked: Made in Italy by Coppola e Toppo
Worn by Ilaria Occhini in *Oggi*, April, 1962, p.51
Barbara Owen Collection, New York

Patrick de Barentzen *tailleur* with button
made exclusively by Coppola e Toppo, 1962
Opaline glass paste spheres mounted as
a cluster on a metal convex beading screen
Published in *Arianna*, May 1962, p.75
Photo: Alfa Castaldi

Ring for Patrick de Barentzen, 1962
Glass paste spheres and conterie mounted on
a gilded metal convex beading screen
Marked: Made in Italy by Coppola e Toppo

Original drawing that accompanied the
design patent request for a button presented
by Coppola e Toppo and Patrick de Barentzen,
Rome, 1962

VIAGGIO DI NOZZE: LONDRA, CANARIE?

Bianco abbagliante, per
un viaggio al Sud, il
tailleur di Patrick De
Barentzen, con la blu-
sa e il grande cappel-
lo alla Boldini di M.
Gilles in shantung ri-
gato bianco e azzurro.

Di Balmain, il giovanis-
simo tailleur in secca
lana giallo pulcino, con
la gonna mossa da
sfondi di piega e la
giacca breve e avvitata.
In seta stampata con
collo-sciarpa la blusa.

In morbida lana a
grandi riquadri scozze-
si bianchi e blu il tail-
leur di Dior con la
gonna a scatola, la giac-
ca corta, la blusa in
crêpe blu con cravat-
ta, la cintura bassa.

d

Un completo insolito e
divertente: è di Jacque-
line de Sthen, la pic-
cola giacca in grosso
pied-de-poule bianco e
blu-grigio è terminata
da un alto bordo nel
tessuto della camicetta.

Di lino azzurro cielo il
tailleur di Patrick De
Barentzen con il col-
letto della giacca for-
mato da tanti petali
ritagliati. Gonna a te-
li. Un grande bottone
di pietre azzurre simi-
le all'unico orecchino.
(Coppola e Toppo).

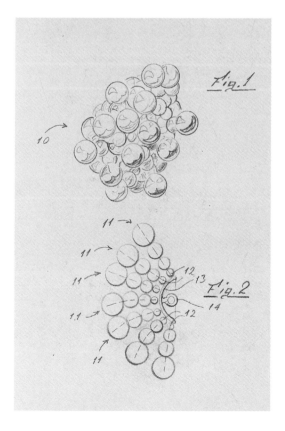

Bolero, 1962
String and weft-mounted plastic
faceted beads forming a square
motif obliquely arranged
Worn by Elsa Martinelli on the
cover of *Voi*, March 1962

VOI

ANNO II - N. 3
MARZO 1962 - L. 200

MODA:
I MODELLI
PIU' RAFFINATI
DEI SEI
PIU' FAMOSI
SARTI DI
PARIGI
E LA
COLLEZIONE
1962 DI
SCHUBERTH
FOTOGRAFATA
NELLA SUA
FAVOLOSA
DIMORA

PAOLO COSTA

Single dangling bunch earring made for
Patrick de Barentzen, 1962
Photographed on a de Barentzen dress
in *Arianna*, March 1962, p.27

Ten-strand necklace for Yves Saint Laurent, 1962
Half-crystal faceted beads alternating with
simulated pearls weft-mounted on the rear
and string-mounted on the front
Marked: Made in Italy by Coppola e Toppo
Published in *Novità*, November 1962, p.61 and
in Mulvagh J., *Costume Jewelry in Vogue*,
Thames and Hudson Inc., New York, 1988, p.126

All the reviews for the de Barentzen collection that appeared in the newspapers of the period were positive and laid emphasis on the beautiful accessories created by Coppola e Toppo. Silvana Bernasconi wrote: "Many new ideas and a good direction in the Patrick de Barentzen fashion parade: high waist, marked by large crystal buttons in the form of a bunch of grapes; tweed pearl-studded *tailleurs*; mysterious fencer-type head-dresses with the face circled by flowers and finally 'jais' boleros, made for him by Coppola e Toppo, masters of fashion jewellery."[33]

In the fashion shows for the 1962/63 winter collection held in July 1962, Coppola e Toppo were again chosen by a large number of designers as suppliers of fashion jewellery and accessories: Lancetti, Baldini and Pucci. The comment by Elisa Massei in *Women's Wear Daily* could not have been more gratifying: "Jewelry made for Lancetti and Emilio Pucci designs is striking."[34]

The success gained in 1962 was crowned by the collaboration with Yves Saint Laurent, who in January that year decided to open his fashion house in Paris, in rue Spuntini.

In the 1960s, even the bags made by Coppola e Toppo enjoyed a great sales success as the fashion tended to smaller, more decorative pieces, as Silvana Bernasconi bore witness: "Enormous bags don't go with the latest fashion. They will be scaled down, they will become smaller and portable, like the form of an envelope or a sachet, folded on itself in soft leather like a glove or even better in velvet. Evening bags are completely in steel-coloured embroidered 'jais' or ruby red".[35]

1962 was therefore a year of great expansion for Coppola e Toppo even in Italy. Silvana Bernasconi wrote: "Such a sophisticated woman will only wear fabulous jewels. In Paris, Cis, in Italy Coppola e Toppo, Fratti and Canesi (our three best *bijoutiers*), have prepared caskets of hard stones and faceted 'jais' to give sparkle to the neck and arms. 'Jais' necklaces as lace *collarettes* with three or four strands of round and bright white pearls, following the fashion launched by Chanel, will underline the charm of the autumn woman."[36]

1963 marked a turning point. Coppola e Toppo jewellery had conquered vast areas of the foreign market, including Australia. Biki, a fashion designer, advocate of Italian style, who also dabbled as a journalist, wrote: "There is a group in Milan making fake jewels that maybe – with the exception of Paris – has no rivals. Speaking personally, I have been a maniac for fake jewellery for years and years, and amongst those creating the jewels for my collections, I've often given preference to Lyda Coppola, an explosive personality with a zest for life. Just in her laboratory of fashion jewellery, a side 'branch' of the fashion industry, there are thirty people working with specialised skills, a person in charge and a complicated administration ... almost as complicated as the one in a large fashion house. In this field too, for that matter, two collections

[33] Bernasconi S., 'Palazzo Pitti ha regalato l'impero alle donne' in *Settimo giorno*, 30 January 1962, p.32
[34] Massei E., 'Jewels of Italy' in *Women's Wear Daily*, 20 July 1962
[35] Bernasconi S., 'Tutte le donne saranno bionde in autunno con un sofisticato "maquillage"' in *La Provincia*, 5 September 1962
[36] Bernasconi S., 'Trucchi di stagione' in *Gazzetta di Reggio*, 8 September 1962

Collar necklace, 1962
String-mounted half-crystal faceted beads and simulated baroque pearls overhanging the underlying weft of half-crystal faceted beads, forming a braid motif
Marked: Made in Italy by Coppola e Toppo
Published in different colours in *Grazia*, December 1962, p.142
The same model was made in a multitude of materials and colours: gilded plastic spheres and simulated baroque pearls, round pearls and black half-crystal faceted beads, crystal beads in contrasting colours, etc.
Paola Bay Collection, Milan

are prepared and shown each year, and buyers gather in this city not only from all of Italy but also from Europe and the rest of the world. That's how Mrs. Toppo keeps in touch with American and Australian cities. I still remember, with the late Jacques Fath, both of them 'lying on their stomachs' in the middle of the salon, getting excited at the idea of launching again on the modern market the fashion of the woman loaded with fake jewels. In this field, the most important factor is colour and the combination of colours. Strange and wild inventions that, in the fine jewellery field, can neither be ventured nor materially made. I have the impression, however, that the vogue for fake jewellery has also started to undermine the rooted conservatism of fine jewellery. The shop windows of the most important jewellers seem to have become more colourful."[37]

As proof of the fact that she preferred Coppola e Toppo jewellery, Biki chose them for her first collection presented in Florence (January 1963), as did Lancetti, Forquet, Enzo, Principessa Borghese and, of course, Pucci. Referring to the outfits of Lancetti, with white as the predominant colour, Irene Brin commented: "Coppola e Toppo have let a stunning river of topaz and amethyst stones flow in their bracelets and necklaces."[38]

An article by Maria Pezzi, in that same year, reporting on a conversation with Lyda, provides an update on the evolution of the company Coppola e Toppo and their relationship with the Italian couturiers: "I don't take care that much of our private customers," Lyda Coppola tells me. She has been living and working

[37] Biki, 'Mille gioielli falsi e belli' in *Corriere Lombardo*, *Tutto Donna*, 13-14 December 1963
[38] Brin I., 'A ogni donna la sua perla' in *Corriere d'informazione*, 23 January 1963

Festoon necklace, 1962
Weft-mounted half-crystal faceted beads and simulated
pearls,conterie, pavé embroidered heart-shaped clasp
Marked: Made in Italy by Coppola e Toppo

Choker, 1962
Half-crystal and plastic faceted beads
mounted on a weft of half-crystal beads
Marked: Made in Italy by Coppola e Toppo
Published in *Successo*, August 1962, p.55
Barbara Owen Collection, New York

Collar necklace, c.1962
Variation of the model shown on p.152
Simulated baroque pearls and gilded
metal spheres pebbled and brushed
Marked: Made in Italy by Coppola e Toppo

Scarf necklace, 1961
Weft-mounted half-crystal faceted beads
Published in different colourway in *Arianna*, December 1961, p.77

Festoon necklace, c.1962
Half-crystal faceted beads mounted to form a sheath on a memory
wire with descending tassels of varying lengths, conterie

Biki portrait with Coppola e
Toppo jewels by Brunetta, c.1963
Pen and ink drawing destined for
publication in *Bellezza*
Signed: Brunetta

Biki portrait by Brunetta, c.1965
Pen and ink drawing
Signed: Brunetta

Flower-shaped brooch, 1962
Weft-mounted half-crystal faceted beads on a brass base
Marked: Made in Italy by Coppola e Toppo
A necklace with the same flower motif was published
in *Classe*, May-June 1962, p.93

Coppola e Toppo dangling earrings worn by
Princess Maria Pia di Savoia on an Emilio Pucci dress
American *Vogue*, November 1963, pp. 108-109

in the fashion business for fifteen years, from the first necklace that so excited Madame Schiaparelli. She is familiar with the needs, the refinements and the tastes of both the Americans as well as the English and French. "Almost all our production goes abroad and since it isn't regular costume jewellery but very special *bijoux de couture*, it goes to the most important designers. Here in Italy, our jewels are sold directly by the fashion houses. Emilio Pucci, for example, is my best client. You could say he is the Italian Chanel. We remake the bows and the *cabochon*-cut crystals necklace in the colours of his jersey outfits by the thousand, just like also some necklaces expressly created for his blouses and his swimming pool-side wear. In the latest issue of *Vogue*[39] there's a huge photograph of Maria Pia di Savoia Karageorgevich wearing a Pucci-designed long velvet dress and the earrings I created in the same colours.

I collaborate very closely with some designers and I study the jewels for them on the basis of the neckline or cut they adopt. The young Lancetti, for example, who this year won the *Critica di Moda* (Fashion critic) award, gives me a series of ideas which I then develop according to my taste and the material I have. Sometimes the crystal necklaces become collars, cuffs, décolleté trimmings or even evening boleros. These are

H.R.H. PRINCESS ALEXANDER OF YUGOSLAVIA
Born Princess Maria-Pia di Savoia, she has warm rosy-beige skin, dark-brown eyes, and famously pretty feet—small, high-arched. She adores sports, particularly swimming and skiing; talks wittily, with a direct charm, in several languages (often enlivening her French with bits of Parisian slang); lives in Versailles with her husband, Prince Alexander, and their two sets of twins—Princes Michel and Dimitri, five; Princess Marie-Hélène and Prince Alexander, under a year. Here, on a recent visit to Italy, she wears Emilio Pucci's black velveteen palazzo pyjamas, edged with scalloping, printed with stained-glass designs in yellow and gold; Pucci's drop earrings. For this photograph, it amused her to wear a big, carved wig by Filippo that completely hid her own chestnut-brown hair. Make-up: Elizabeth Arden's Roman Salon, by Pablo. Pyjamas at Saks Fifth Avenue.

[39] American *Vogue*, 1 November 1963, pp. 108-109

jewels that require an enormous amount of work and a choice of materials that is huge in terms of colours and shades. Of course, not everyone understands these jewels that are not at all imitations of fine jewellery but have instead a very precise decorative function and must be aggressive, imaginative, eccentric. They become chic and valuable on a mountain sweater or on a sponge shirt rather than at *La Scala*. Naturally I also have a 'quieter' production, more suitable to all women. In America, this year, the *collarette* (collar necklace) that imitates a large *ajour* (open-work) has been the most popular. For women who spend most of their time in sweaters and knitted garments, this is the ideal jewel".[40]

Coppola e Toppo also created jewels for Pucci's outfits, and it is interesting to read the comments made by a great writer, Dino Buzzati, who spent a few years "loaned out" to the fashion world: "This year Pucci has found his inspiration in Polynesia and the result we saw last night was irresistible for the physical joy that so many marvellous colours, stunningly displayed, provided. Describing them is practically absurd. Wave after wave of increasing gaiety and vividness, like standing in front of a display of fireworks ..."[41]

Again in 1963, Coppola e Toppo took part in a handicraft exhibition promoted in London by the *Istituto Italiano per il Commercio Estero* (Italian Institute for Foreign Trade), that was presenting the best of 'Made in Italy' high-quality craftsmanship, from shoes to gloves, from silk to fashion jewellery.

In 1964, Italy was struck by a strong economic recession. Employment of women was particularly hit, falling dramatically but then picking up again over the next few years with the rise of work at home. Companies, which had concentrated production on the factory floor until then, began redirecting production by distributing work to cottage industries. As a result of the violent union demands, culminating in the "hot autumn" of 1969, the cost of labour increased significantly and so the competition with other markets, Britain amongst these, became increasingly tougher. With women and young people unemployed on the one hand, and the request for greater productivity and commitment to workers on the other, the possibility of a crisis in the world of high fashion began to loom. Bruno and Lyda, while continuing to collaborate with the major fashion designers such as Lancetti, decided to open an office/show-room in the historical centre of Milan, in via Manzoni, 20, opposite where the Armani store is today. The office was soon transformed into a veritable boutique. This move sprang perhaps from the need to ward off the recession that was in the air, and, at the same time, take advantage of the tendency that was seeing the high fashion atelier replaced by young trendy boutiques, where miniskirts and Courrèges boots reigned. Another major event in that year was that Lyda Toppo became the artistic consultant for Daniel Swarovski Corporation from Wattens, the world's largest manufacturer of imitation stones, a position she held until 1972.

The management at Swarovski entrusted Lyda with the responsibility of preparing a collection of fashion jewels made exclusively with their stones and interpreting a totally new development, the *Florentine Carré*, a highly gleaming *carré*-cut stone, whose facets showed iridescent reflections like the wings of dragonflies and scarabs.

For the first time in the history of Italian high fashion parades, a fashion show exclusively dedicated to fashion jewellery and accessories was organised by Coppola e Toppo at Palazzo Pitti on 20 July. Their jewellery was worn on jersey outfits designed by Pucci and Lancetti.

The management of her boutique and the artistic consultancy for Daniel Swarovski did not prevent Lyda from working as she had in the past with the Italian couturiers. In January 1964, Coppola e Toppo fashion jewellery accompanied the collections of Lancetti (Lyda created boleros with half-crystal beads for him), Pucci, Biki, Enzo, de Barentzen, Marucelli, Principessa Borghese and Glans.

In commenting on the last day of the fashion shows for the 1964-65 autumn/winter collections presented in Florence, Irene Brin wrote: "Coppola e Toppo have shown that you can protect yourself magnificently from the rain with a diamond-studded umbrella. They have shown us everything. *Colliers de chien*, tiaras, bonnets, wigs, sandals, shoes, big bags, holdalls, suitcases, tops, corsets, cuffs, bracelets, rings, flounces, scarves, combs... Have I forgotten anything that can be

[40] Pezzi M., 'I falsi raffinati della fantasia' in *Il Giorno*, 8 December 1963
[41] Buzzati D., 'E' il viola la tinta di moda' in *Corriere della Sera*, 19 September 1963

Necklace with calla motif, c.1961
String-mounted half-crystal faceted beads
forming the front and weft-mounted half-crystal
beads forming the rear of the necklace
Marked: Made in Italy by Coppola e Toppo
A necklace with calla motif but a different front
was pubblished in *Arianna*, August 1961, p.12
Brett Benson Collection, Chicago

studded with gems??? Well, if I have, Coppola e Toppo certainly have not, and were acclaimed for a full fifteen minutes and with the typical excitement that comes from the sight of so much lustre."[42]

In October, Coppola e Toppo and Fontana Calzature (Fontana shoes) were elected as the representatives of accessory manufacturers on the board of directors for the *Camera Nazionale della Moda Italiana,* located in Rome, for the two-year period 1964-65.

1965 appeared to be a year of "specialisation" rather than one of innovation. No revolutionary ideas emerged from the fashion shows in Florence and Rome as the designers concentrated rather on the cut and finishing techniques.

Coppola e Toppo also did not turn out any new ideas but limited themselves to retouching their pre-existing models, and at the fashion shows in Rome in 1965 their jewellery accompanied just the outfits of Carosa, Ken Scott and Jole Veneziani. In the months that followed, the boutique in Milan enjoyed major success with customers whose individual needs required particular attention. It was for this reason then that Lyda began to sacrifice her collaborative ventures with the fashion designers, with one major exception, Valentino Garavani. This young designer had made his début adopting the name Valentino in Florence at the *Sala Bianca* with his autumn/winter collection 1960-1961. Valentino's talent was immediately recognised in the United States before gaining acknowledgement in Italy. From the very first time they met in 1964,

Jacqueline Kennedy became his most important client, and a friend shortly thereafter, followed by the Ford sisters, Mrs. William B. Paley and Jacqueline De Ribes. In Italy, the 'First Lady' Marella Agnelli was one of his most devoted admirers.

In July 1965, Valentino presented his collection, accompanied by Coppola e Toppo jewellery, which was so extraordinary that *Women's Wear Daily* had a huge banner headline: "Fabulous Italy!"[43]

This first success marked the start of an association that would result in the triumph, especially on the American market, for Valentino and his outfits accompanied by Coppola e Toppo jewellery, bags and belts, for day wear and evening wear. The penetration of the Coppola e Toppo products into the international market appeared to be gaining ground, perhaps, as Maria Pezzi maintains, because of the lack of any major competition. With regard to the collections of Italian high fashion paraded in Rome in January 1966, Maria Pezzi wrote: "It's strange how in Italy, where boutiques increase in number thick and fast and where imagination is certainly not lacking, there are so few designers of fashion accessories. Since the start of the fashion shows in Florence, the designers have always been the same. Amongst them, one of the best known names is Coppola e Toppo. Every year they supply an increasing number of fashion houses and boutiques. This year's collection is varied more than ever: positively liberty-style and aggressive jewels for the Emilio Pucci collection; enormous crystal *boules* and *semiboules,* to

be worn barefooted between the toes, for Ognibene-Zendman; a new very light gilded material, mixed with multicoloured coral stones for Mila Schön. The ultra-modern jewels created for the Castillo *tricot* boutique, all made with black and white *baguettes*-cut stones with large *cabochon*-cut crystals of varying colours."[44]

In the meantime, in the second half of the 1960s, many women, even if unconnected with the world of high fashion or luxury ready-made outfits, chose plastic disc earrings, gigantic rings, bracelets and necklaces made with real flowers, necklaces consisting of large spheres. In the wake of the wave of dissent against the traditional values of a capitalist society that swept through the West during the late '60s and 1970s, the result was a subsequent "wanting-to-look-young" mentality from mothers who tried to integrate themselves in their children's noisy and colourful culture. Even the fashion designers came into line and, at the end of the high fashion shows in Rome in January 1966, Irene Brin wrote an article with the following subtitle: "The ideal woman for fashion designers today seems to be a schoolgirl in a leotard, a straight and thin teenager, a young girl. Heading towards the nursery school!"[45] And in the same vein, Lyda Toppo reported in an interview: "It's the daughters that pick the accessory and the mothers who meekly accept; here [her boutique] it's like being at the psychologist's and it's not easy getting these young ladies to change their mind. They always want the strongest and most violent earrings."[46]

Demi-parure made up of necklace and earrings, 1962
String-mounted glass paste spheres and interspersed with
simulated pearls weft-mounted on a rigid 'V' motif
Marked: Made in Italy by Coppola e Toppo
Published in *Women's Wear Daily*, 1 July 1962

In 1967 the youth protest became increasingly bitter, and started to extend to all social levels. The fashion operators fell into line by going slightly more down-market, presenting in the renowned Palazzo Pitti – in April and October rather than January and July – boutique outfits and knitwear together with 'Alta moda pronta' ('ready-made *haute couture*' – a name that of course is a contradiction in terms as, by definition, *haute couture* is made-to-measure, so cannot also be ready-made).

Most probably, faced with the decline of fashion aimed at the select few, Coppola e Toppo focused on retail sales from its shop. The novelty for the year seemed to be represented by a collection of fashion jewellery in multicoloured plastic beads mounted on a memory wire, similar to mattress springs, with a spiral motif wrapped around the neck and the cuffs or dangling harmoniously from the ears.

As far as collaboration with the major fashion designers was concerned, Lyda Toppo chose to work exclusively with Valentino, who in 1967 received the Neiman Marcus award. One of the most inspired ideas this young designer had, was to grant licences for the use of his trademark initials, one of the first logos in the history of fashion. In fact in 1966, belts, ties, bags and *pochette*s with the 'V' symbol were already appearing all over the world. Interestingly enough, it seems that the 'V' was the idea of Lyda, who picked it up from her pieces with the rigid 'V' motif (see the necklace right) produced years before and made the

[42] Brin I., 'Gioielli come se piovesse' in *Corriere d'informazione*, 22 September 1964
[43] *Women Wear Daily*, 23 July 1965
[44] Pezzi M., 'Anelli fino a metà mano' in *Il Giorno*, 16 January 1966
[45] Brin I., 'Ora tutte ragazzine' in *Corriere d'informazione*, 21-22 January 1966
[46] Clerici M.T., 'Scelgono le madri l'accessorio violento' in *Il Giorno*, 29 December 1966

Necklace, perhaps for Emilio Pucci, c.1962
Half-crystal faceted beads mounted in graduated
strings fixed to the underlying weft of beads,
pavé-embroidered heart-shaped clasp
Marked: Made in Italy by Coppola e Toppo
This model, made in autumnal colours, appeared for
the first time in *Women's Wear Daily*, 19 June 1959

relevant adjustments following indications from Valentino, for whom thousands of specimens were then produced with different materials and colours. Marina Cosi wrote: "When in 1966 Valentino launched the famous 'V' – creating a bridge between Consuelo Crespi, Farah Diba, Jacqueline Kennedy and all the *prima donna* that wore Valentino high fashion, on the one hand, and the shop assistants that were gifting ties with the 'V' logo to their boyfriends, on the other – there was a chorus of disapproval so strong to obscured the sky. It was not long however before the other fashion designers stopped disapproving. They were too busy copying Valentino Garavani on the lucrative license business."[47]

For the Valentino autumn/winter collection 1967-1968, presented in Rome in July and in New York in September 1967, Coppola e Toppo created fashion jewellery that was incredibly new, graphic and sculptural, conceived to enrich and embellish the outfit rather than the décolleté. The materials used in the jewellery were no longer half-crystal beads but white, or red, blue, tortoiseshell-like plastic and small aluminium tubes plated in silver or gold, and anodised in cobalt blue, fire red, brown. Together with the fashion jewels, Coppola e Toppo also produced belts, bags and buttons, all with the 'V' for Valentino in gilded or silver plated metal. The artefacts made by Coppola e Toppo for this designer carry a nameplate in metal with the inscription "Coppola e Toppo per Valentino". It was one of the first times in fashion history that the name of the manufacturer was indicated together with the name of the couturier who had inspired and ordered the piece.

The newspaper *Oakland Tribune* commented on an alligator bag with thin V-shaped gilded metal handles: "Lyda Coppola has designed 'the bag of the year' for Valentino. It's been ordered by Jacqueline Kennedy, Lady Astor, Mrs Samuel Reed, one of the Du Pont ladies, the Countess Volpe and the list could go on forever."[48]

In a photographic sequence taken on the occasion of her visit to Italy in November 1967, Jacqueline Kennedy appeared with one of these alligator bags with thin V-shaped gilded metal handles.[49] She appeared again in evening wear with a small gilded tubes and *roses montées pochette* made by Coppola e Toppo for Valentino (see p220-221) on 13 May, 1975 at the Metropolitan Opera House. Many years later, at the preview of the *Jacqueline Kennedy: the White House Years* exhibition held at the Metropolitan Museum on 23 April, 2001, her daughter Caroline was holding the same model of pochette but in silver plated tubes.

The student protest that began in Paris in May 1968 and saw student and workers united in their struggle, ended with the victory of the right-wing parties at the elections that were called after the protest. Despite the political defeat, the students' movement left a deep scar on Western society, especially on women.

Their claims dated back to the beginning of the 1800s, but it was not until the 1960s that, under the banner of feminism, sizeable groups of women radically modified their objectives and fighting methods in their battle for equality. Now that the right to vote had been obtained practically everywhere, the feminist struggle concentrated on the 'private' sphere, and this was also expressed through an 'alternative' way of dressing and behaving. The designers of fashion, however, did not seem to be aware of what was happening in the real world and pursued their business of creating luxury, comfort and elegance for a small elite.

In terms of Italian fashion, the most important event in 1968 was Valentino's *Collezione bianca* (White Collection) for the summer, presented in January in Rome in his sophisticated atelier in via Gregoriana 24: straight miniskirts, high boots, and outfits, coats, *robe-manteaux* (all rigorously white, in twenty different shades, complete with white shoes and stockings, all from Valentino), that through stratagems involving the neckline, stitching, cuts, seams, drew attention towards the letter 'V'. The 'byzantine belts', high and very precious, and the fashion jewels, both the work of Coppola e Toppo, are what everyone noticed on these outfits. And it was Coppola e Toppo again who provided the belts in coloured crystal beads for the *tailleurs* designed by Forquet.

In the fashion shows held at Palazzo Pitti in April 1968, for the autumn/winter collections 1968-1969, Valentino presented evening wear accompanied by the most incredible pectoral jewels from Coppola e Toppo made from small gilded or silver plated tubes, or painted in colours taken from the fabrics, black, blue, red, golden brown. These tubes were all strung together in such a way as to create floral leaf patterns, the borders of which were heightened by *roses montées* glittering with diamond-like light. This was one of the most extraordinary models ever produced in the history of fashion jewellery, an important element in the dressing of Valentino's ideal woman whom he defined in a few words: "A woman must take the breath away when she enters a room. And this is, and will always be, the starting point and final purpose of my evening gowns."[50]

During those same fashion shows, Coppola e Toppo were present as suppliers of jewellery for Krizia – one of the first 'Made in Italy' designers, already famous at the time, who soon after preferred Milan to Florence for the presentation of her designs – as well as half-crystal beads cufflinks for Eguzquiza, a company based in Milan that rapidly left the scene.

Still in 1968, together with outfits made with multicoloured printed fabrics, Coppola e Toppo flip-flop sandals with leather soles appeared for the first time in the fashion magazines. They were made for Emilio Pucci and some footwear companies, Guido Pasquali amongst them, and consisted of a shower of plastic-faceted beads in colours matching the fabric tones.

In the ready-to-wear fashion shows in November 1968 in Florence – where since 1967 only boutique

[47] Cosi M., *Valentino che veste di nuovo*, Camunia, 1984, p.39
[48] 'The bag', *Oakland Tribune*, 5 October 1967
[49] *Gente*, 1 November 1967, front cover
[50] Cosi M., *ibid*, p. 124

Jabot necklace, 1962
String and weft-mounted half-crystal and
plastic faceted beads
Marked: Made in Italy
Published in *Women's Wear Daily*, 1 June 1962
Barbara Owen Collection, New York

collections and high fashion knitwear had been parading – 'gypsy-looking' (as proposed by Ken Scott) women paraded Coppola e Toppo faceted and highly-coloured necklaces and bracelets. The photos of these extravagant outfits, made by Gian Paolo Barbieri, were taken up by many news magazines, such as *L'Europeo*,[51] a weekly that had rarely expressed an interest in fashion trends, but had, in this case, probably understood the spectacular nature of the photographed outfits and accessories.

Again in 1968, Lyda Coppola created three bikinis, made entirely of glass stones, veritable body jewellery, that were so extraordinary that even *Panorama* published them.[52] The reporters, using their imagination, gave the three bikinis exotic names, derived from ancient costumes: one, made of Swarovski 'Margarita' crystals kept together by small glass tubes, was called *cotta*, the coat of chain-mail worn by Barbarossa's warriors; the second, made from just crystal stones mounted as a weft to form the briefs and a stay-up bra, was called *trikini*; the third, *crociata* (crusade), was inspired by the Middle Ages, and made of very thin crystal strips on which were placed the *Florentine Carrés* from Swarovski, a stone that Lyda had contributed in launching in the Florence fashion shows in 1964.

After 1968, the fashion magazines, in particular Italian *Vogue* and *Linea Italiana,* tried to increase their audience by publishing photographs that were new, innovative, unusual, and creative, expressly produced in a studio for their exclusive reports, for which the first models in the history of Italian fashion were engaged. There was Veruschka, a German girl who had moved to Italy, and the Italian Isa Stoppi, Mirella Petteni, Ivana Bastianello and many others. Lyda Toppo enthusiastically took to creating fashion jewels and objects that were conceived for photographic shoots, especially when the photographer involved was Gian Paolo Barbieri, who first became a friend of Lyda's and then almost an adopted son.

The association between this extraordinary fashion photographer – whose work was presented in 2007 by the Municipality of Milan in a retrospective exhibition – and Lyda Toppo is testified by the countless photographic reports made between 1965, the year Gian Paolo Barbieri embarked on his career as a fashion photographer, and 1977. For Gian Paolo Barbieri's shoots, Lyda also created some experimental pieces of jewellery. These were not meant to be put into production, and nowadays look often unrecognisable as Coppola e Toppo next to the company's marketed jewels, initially classic in their form and then, as time

went on, more graphic and sculptural.

Amongst the jewels expressly created for the shoots and then actually made for just a few important women, the necklace *Fuochi d'artificio* (Fireworks) stands out. It was conceived by Lyda Toppo and used for various photo shoots paired with the outfits of several designers (Mila Schön, Lancetti, Valentino); it has become a cult object for collectors of vintage *bijoux de couture*.

Finally the real world caught up with the fashion world and the force of the youth protest and the rage of the feminist movement left their mark – the high fashion collections held in January 1969 were not a success, neither with the public, nor with the buyers. Even the collection presented by Valentino – whose fame seemed to be able to overcome any crisis – both in Rome and in New York, was only tepidly received, and in some cases indeed criticised as lacking coherence.[53]

Instead, there was just praise and approval for the Coppola e Toppo jewellery accompanying the Valentino outfits, amongst which a piece of jewellery with one of the greatest impacts ever made: a necklace of rectangular rhinestones in contrasting colours (blue and white, yellow and topaz, shocking pink and pale pink) separated by metal bars mounted in such a way

as to form one or three broad circles.

Talking about the high fashion shows presented in Rome of the January that year, Silvana Bernasconi said: "Of the three to four thousand outfits presented in these collections, let's mention the best-sellers: the de Barentzen trouser-suit, the Valentino-designed *redingote* with blue and white tropical flowers and embroidered stockings, and Coppola e Toppo coral stars and diamonds..."[54]

The buckles and jewellery created by Coppola e Toppo for Antonelli, based on a bamboo wood motif, also enjoyed reasonable success.

The Coppola e Toppo jewellery pieces that accompanied the Gattinoni autumn/winter collection 1969/1970 were basically remakes of the famous models made of small tubes a year earlier for Valentino with the addition of coloured plexiglass flowers.

[51] 'Le zingare dell'alta moda' in *L'Europeo*, 9 May 1968
[52] 'Balocchi di cristallo e fantasia per ballare sotto la luna' *Panorama*, 18 May 1968
[53] Pezzi M., 'Valentino-maratona a corrente alternata' in *Il Giorno*, 21 January 1969
[54] Bernasconi S., 'Alle sfilate di Roma un ritorno alla natura' in *Il giornale di Brescia*, 30 January 1969

The start of the 1970s seemed to coincide with a major about turn. The specialist fashion magazines were becoming thicker and heavier because each designer (Antonelli, Capucci, Sorelle Fontana, Jole Veneziani, Barocco, Heinz Riva, Curiel, Carosa, André Laug, Mila Schön, Forquet and others) were buying page after page of advertising to then be compensated by long editorial articles, dedicated not surprisingly to the trade names that were appearing in the same magazines as advertisers. The mentions of the 'old and famous' fashion jewellery manufacturers such as Coppola e Toppo, Fratti, Canesi, Cis had disappeared from the specialised press, substituted by the names of the new generation of jewellery makers: Borbonese, Ugo Correani, Sharra Pagano, Bozart, the American Kenneth J. Lane, distributed in Italy by Ferragamo.

Even the old-guard couturiers were being replaced by new personalities, the designers, who would deservedly become the stars of 'Made in Italy' fashion.

During this period, Lyda Toppo was closely involved with the running of her boutique. As well as offering fashion jewellery, bags, handbags, suitcases, foulards, scarves and blouses (which were now made according to her designs by external workshops), the boutique was also selling ornaments that were not her creations. She collaborated with Ken Scott for his autumn/winter collection 1970-1971 and also dedicated herself to designing household objects – all with carved surfaces deriving from bronze or brass casts – such as small sculptures, lamps, wine racks, ice bucket sets, cigarette cases and lighter holders, closable ashtrays, vases, and umbrella stands. In 1971, *Oggi*, a widely read weekly magazine, published a long interview under the banner headline: "Women who have changed Italian taste: Lyda Coppola, creator of fashion jewellery". It was the consecration of her fame in Italy. In France, America, Canada, Britain and even in Australia, she had been famous for over twenty years.

In the interview, Lyda Coppola advised how and which pieces of jewellery to wear, a guideline which, in my opinion, is still valid today:

"Being elegant does not necessarily mean wearing very valuable jewels or clothes. There are women of modest means who know how to be far more elegant than those who wear made-to-measure designer outfits."

"Accessories are extremely important because they reveal the personality of a woman."

"The basic rule with jewels is 'too much deforms'. You can go as far as you like in regards to the strength of the piece, the originality of the design, the colour, but never in quantity. Too many jewels are good for a circus parade, but do not make you look elegant."

"You can wear fine jewels only when you go to the opening of *La Scala* or at a wedding. For any other occasion, it's better to leave them in the vault, to forget them, especially the pearl necklace. Any woman wearing it looks automatically twenty years behind the times."

"The more important the jewel is, the more it needs to stand alone."

"It is always necessary to create a separation, an empty space between one jewel and another. When the necklace makes a statement, no earrings; when the earring is important, no necklace, maybe a bracelet."

"When the outfit is important, never load it down with jewels. One only, but classy, is enough."

"When the outfit is made with a printed fabric, you need a jewel to go perfectly with the colour or colours of the fabric. Otherwise it's better not to wear anything."

"When the outfit is simple or plain-coloured, you can wear a few more accessories: necklace, earrings, bracelet; but watch out for the colour matching."

"Remember that a piece of costume jewellery will never be an ornament to go with everything. It will be perfect for a particular outfit, or at best, for a group of outfits."

"For the day dress, I advise just small earrings, not too visible, or else a necklace."

"For a lunch meeting, earrings and a necklace."

"For the afternoon, you can add one or two extra items, or even better, substitute a simple jewel with a slightly more important one."

"For the evening, you can increase the number of

Collar necklace, perhaps for Emilio Pucci, 1963
String-mounted multicoloured plastic faceted beads fixed
to an underlying weft of transparent halt-crystal beads
Marked: Made in Italy by Coppola e Toppo
Published in *Women's Wear Daily*, 14 June 1963
Pauline Gasbarro Collection, New York

jewels, especially in the summer. For a long evening gown, a lot depends on the cut of the dress because the jewel has to highlight its style. I suggest long necklaces if the outfit is flowing, collar necklaces if the line of the outfit is elaborate."

"The belt is never worn with long and important necklaces. If the necklace is short, then the belt can also be prominent."

"Bracelets can be worn with earrings, but you can never have earrings, bracelets and necklaces. Only a long dress (or a special occasion) can sustain that combination. As a rule, you should only wear two jewels, very rarely three. If the outfit demands it, you can have a brooch instead of a necklace. For example, bracelet, earrings and brooch."[55]

Despite having appeared on various pages of one of the best and most widely-read illustrated magazines in Italy and another fruitful collaboration with Lancetti in 1971, by 1972 Lyda started to become prone to cyclical bouts of depression. She stopped devoting herself to design and creativity, with the exception of some erratic intrusions into the world of design, painting and poetry. It was no coincidence that 1972 was also the year in which it became clear to everyone that *prêt-à-porter* was rapidly substituting high fashion, the latter now reserved to just a few thousand women throughout the world. From 1972 to 1976, Coppola e Toppo fashion jewels were very rarely appearing in

[55] Fogliani, P., *ibid*

the specialised magazines and when they did, they looked like variations of models already seen in previous years.

Lyda spent ten years in pain suffering with illness. In 1982, poetry verses that she had started writing in 1979, were published in the anthology *Una Strada* (A Road) in a limited edition of 120 numbered copies. The poems raised the curtain on her personal life, and in particular on her unhappy childhood. As you read the words written by this woman, whose creativity was lauded throughout the world and who was awarded with fame and success, it is surprising to find yourself looking at painful memories of a sad childhood. Memories which she had apparently managed to repress only by constant commitment to her work, to which she said she dedicated her life. Lyda writes of the suffering of her mother, abandoned by her husband when their three children were still very young; of the economic shortages of a family in which her mother had taken up the father-figure role and an aunt that of the mother; and of the loneliness, the sacrifices and the pain that followed the abandonment. The international fame gained by Lyda in the years that followed and the recognition she achieved with the public and her colleagues, were not enough to make her forget the painful past. After years of unrestrained and uninterrupted activity, something had cracked inside her. In these cases, nobody can ever say what triggered this result, whether it was an inevitable illness or her inability to accept that her world, made up of elegance, luxury, discretion, *bon ton*, which she had entirely conquered thanks to her talent and her sense of beauty, had changed so quickly and without giving her the time to adapt. Her absence from the whirl of the fashion had been too long and she herself wrote: "Too much time had passed, too many things had changed. I wasn't useful anymore."

On 15 February, 1986, in Milan, Lyda Coppola died as a result of multiple serious illnesses.[56] Her funeral, which was conducted according to Jewish rites, was attended only by a few personal friends.

[56] The management of the Coppola e Toppo shop passed onto Bruno Coppola's son, Sandro Coppola, who focused activities on the sale of fashion jewellery and accessories by many manufacturers up until 1990, when a Biella-based company took over the shop. In 1996 the Coppola e Toppo premises were taken up by Pellini Fashion Jewellery, thus providing a third point of sale in Milan.

Donatella Pellini, famous – not only in Italy but also abroad – began designing fashion jewellery in 1972, at the dawn of the 'Made in Italy' period. In 1974 she began her infinite and innovative working of the resin she applies to her ornaments. With the advent of Pellini Bijoux it seems that destiny has provided an ideal way for the great tradition of Coppola e Toppo to continue. Donatella Pellini, a skilled and innovative designer, is responsible for the design and realisation of fashion jewels that are just as famous as the Coppola e Toppo ones, though "modern" expressions of their era and, perhaps, worthy of a book in their own right.

Bib necklace, c.1964
Weft-mounted half-crystal faceted beads on the rear part
and string-mounted on the front
Marked: Made in Italy by Coppola e Toppo
Published in different colours in *Gioia*, October 1964, p.55
Chisa Kotaki Collection, Tokyo

In the photo the model is wearing a hair bandana and a belt made by Coppola e Toppo with Swarovski "Florentine Carré" stones for their fashion show at Palazzo Pitti, Florence, 20 July 1964

Model with silk umbrella studded with Swarovski
"Margarita" crystals by Coppola e Toppo
for their fashion show at Palazzo Pitti, Florence,
20 July 1964

Lustred faceted crystal cylinders mounted to form
a weft on which Swarovski "Margarita" crystals are sewn
Marked: Made in Italy by Coppola e Toppo
Published in *Bellezza*, December 1964, p.38
An identical necklace is part of the permanent collection of
jewellery at the Musée des Arts Décoratifs in Paris, donated
in 2004 by Barbara Berger after the exhibition of her collection
of fashion jewellery at the Musée de la Mode e du Textile
accompanied by the catalogue *Luxe et Fantaisie*, Norma
Editions, Paris, 2003

Tie-necklace, 1964
Weft-mounted faceted half-crystal beads with Swarovski
"Margarita" crystal in graduated measure mounted above
Published in *Bellezza*, September 1964, p.40
Marion Stern Collection, Paris

Collar necklace, 1964
Weft-base made in half-crystal faceted transparent beads
on which Swarovski "Margarita" crystals are applied
Marked: Made in Italy by Coppola e Toppo
Irma Barni Castiglioni Collection, Milan

Collar necklace, 1964
Weft-base made in half-crystal faceted transparent beads
on which Swarovski "Margarita" crystals are applied
Marked: Made in Italy by Coppola e Toppo
Private Collection, Pisa

177

Graduated semi-sphere necklace with central pendant, 1964
Weft-mounted half-crystal faceted beads forming semi-sphere
motifs overlapped by Swarovski "Margarita" crystals
Marked: Made in Italy by Coppola e Toppo
Published in green colourway in *Bellezza*, September 1964, p.27
Barbara Berger Collection, Mexico City

Graduated semi-sphere necklace, 1964
Weft-mounted half-crystal faceted beads forming semi-sphere
motifs overlapped by Swarovski "Margarita" crystals
Marked: Made in Italy by Coppola e Toppo
Published in green colourway in *Bellezza*,
September 1964, p.27

Rossana Schiaffino wearing Coppola e Toppo
jewellery in *Oggi*, 20 February 1968, p.45
(photographer unknown)
The necklace was also published in *Grazia*,
2 August 1964, p.37

Dangling earrings, 1964
Graduated string-mounted Swarovski lustred crystal
cylinders and "Margarita" crystals, pavé embroidered
Marked: Made in Italy by Coppola e Toppo

NA FRANGIA DI CRISTALLO Roma. L'argento è il tono do
nciatura studiata dal visagista Gil per Rosanna Schiaffino: nero, azzurro
argento sono le sfumate tonalità del trucco; e d'argento opaco i nei cospar
sulle gote. In cristallo argentato, infine, sono i gioielli di Coppola e Toppo

Festoon necklace, 1964
Graduated string-mounted Swarovski faceted
lustred crystal cylinders fixed on a weft of
half-crystal faceted transparent beads
Marked: Made in Italy by Coppola e Toppo
Published in *Successo*, June 1967, p.139

Bib necklace with floral motifs, 1964
Faceted Swarovski lustred crystal cylinders mounted
to form flowers in the centre of which a Swarovski
"Margarita" crystal is applied
A brooch in the same form is published in *Linea*,
winter 1964, p.29

The model Isa Stoppi photographed by
Gian Paolo Barbieri with a Coppola e Toppo
necklace, Milan, 1965

Necklace with central loop motifs, c.1965
String-mounted pure crystal and lustred half-crystal
faceted beads, Swarovski "Margarita" crystals, conterie
Marked: Made in Italy
Private Collection, Pisa

Necklace with candy motifs, c.1965
String and weft-mounted half-crystal faceted
beads, pavé-embroidered heart-shaped clasp
Marked: Coppola Toppo

Leaf branches necklace, 1964
Half-crystal faceted beads weft-mounted to form leaf
motifs fixed to a sheath in weft-mounted half-crystal beads
covering a plastic tube with inside a memory wire
The same model in pink was published in American *Vogue*,
December 1964, p.210 and in *Linea*, autumn 1964, p.44

Eight-strand necklace made for Emilio Pucci, c.1965
String-mounted half-crystal faceted beads mounted on an
underlying weft of beads, pavé-embroidered heart-shaped clasp
Marked: Made in Italy by Coppola e Toppo
Private Collection, Pisa

Demi-parure made up of single-strand necklace with cascading
central motif and button earrings, 1964
Half-crystal faceted beads mounted on segments of rigid annealed
wire fixed on an underlying weft of transparent plastic
The necklace was published in *New York Times Magazine*, 2 August 1964
A version in grey/azure tones is published in Farneti Cera, D. (ed.), *I gioielli
della fantasia*, Idea Books, Milan, 1991, p.280

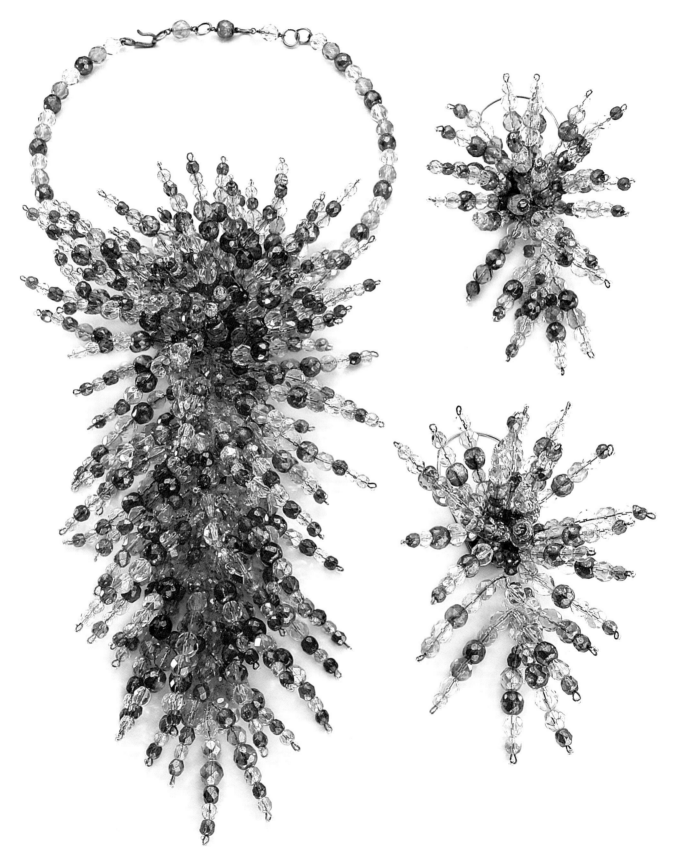

Collar necklace, perhaps for Emilio Pucci, 1964
Half-crystal faceted beads overlapping a weft of half-crystal beads
Marked: Made in Italy by Coppola e Toppo
Published in *Novità*, May 1964, p.48

Collar necklace, 1964
Glass paste spheres mixed with polished and brushed
metal 'boules' mounted on a weft of half-crystal beads
Marked: Made in Italy by Coppola e Toppo
Published in *Women's Wear Daily*, 1 June 1964

Necklace with ajour (open-work) motif, 1964
String and weft-mounted half-crystal and plastic faceted beads
Marked: Made in Italy by Coppola e Toppo
Published in *Women's Wear Daily*, 1 June 1964

Necklace, perhaps for Ken Scott, c.1965
Plastic faceted beads mounted on a weft of plastic beads
Marked: Made in Italy by Coppola e Toppo

Isa Stoppi photographed by Gian Paolo Barbieri,
c.1965 wearing the bracelet from a set with the
necklace shown below

Pectoral necklace, c.1965
Weft-mounted half-crystal faceted beads forming
leaf motifs fixed to a base of plastic beads
Marked: Coppola Toppo
Leila Marzagao Collection, London

'Aztec' necklace with graduated festoons, 1965
Lustred crystal faceted cylinders and Swarovski "Margarita" crystals
Marked: Made in Italy by Coppola e Toppo
Published in *Vogue Novità*, March 1966, p.99
Unger Collection, Milan

The model Donyale Luna with Coppola e Toppo jewels
photographed by Gian Paolo Barbieri for Italian *Vogue*,
November 1966, p.66-67

Sautoir with central flower-shaped pendant
for Ken Scott, second half of the 1960s
String mounted half-crystal faceted beads for the chain and
string-mounted plastic beads fixed on a weft for the pendant
Paolo Bay Collection, Milan

The same necklaces with flower-shaped pendant published
above are worn as a bikini by Marina Schiano, photographed
by Gian Paolo Barbieri, second half of the 1960s
Photo published in Faccioli, D., Barbieri, G.P., Chitolina, A.,
Gian Paolo Barbieri, A History of Fashion, Photology, Milan, 2002,
pp.170-171

200

Sautoir with central flower-shaped pendant for
Ken Scott, second half of the 1960s
Half-crystal faceted beads for the chain and string-
mounted plastic beads fixed on a weft for the pendant
Donatella Pellini Collection, Milan

Demi-parure made up of necklace and dangling earrings
made for Ken Scott, 1969
Half-crystal and plastic faceted beads mounted in graduated strings fixed
to the underlying weft of beads, pavé-embroidered heart-shaped clasp
Marked on earrings and necklance: Made in Italy by Coppola e Toppo
Published in *Grazia*, 2 February 1969, p.42, paired with a Ken Scott outfit
Earrings: Barbara Owen Collection, New York

Bib necklace with triangle motif, 1965
String and weft-mounted half-crystal faceted beads
Marked: Made in Italy by Coppola e Toppo
Published in *Gioia*, 21 April 1965, p.65

Choker, c. 1967
Half-crystal faceted beads, brushed and
polished gilded metal spheres
Marina Gregotti Collection, Milan

Experimental jewels created by Lyda Coppola
photographed by Gian Paolo Barbieri for
Linea Italiana, autumn/winter 1966-67, p.52

Model wearing an outfit on which are fixed
experimental jewels made by Lyda Coppola with
potatoes soaked in a Wood lamp reagent
photographed by Gian Paolo Barbieri for *Linea Italiana*,
autumn/winter 1966-67, p.53

Mirella Petteni wearing a Coppola e Toppo bracelet
photographed by Gian Paolo Barbieri
for *L'Europeo*, 9 May 1968, p.91

Demi-parure made up of choker and dangling earrings, 1967
Faceted plastic beads mounted on a memory wire
Marked on necklace: Coppola Toppo
Published in Italian *Vogue*, July 1967, p.18
Earrings published in Italian *Vogue*, June 1967, p.46

Bracelet, c. 1966
Weft-mounted half-crystal faceted beads,
pavé-embroidered brass clasp
Marked on clasp: Made in Italy by Coppola e Toppo

Two single dangling earrings, 1966
Weft-mounted plastic faceted beads forming
a loop-shaped faceted transparent beaded sheath
Marked on brass clip: Made in Italy by Coppola e Toppo
Published in different colours in *I a Donna*, December 1966, p.60
Donatella Pellini Collection, Milan

210

Nine-strand bracelet, 1967
Faceted plastic beads, gilded plastic boules,
pavé-embroidered rectangular clasp
Marked: Made in Italy by Coppola e Toppo
Published in *La Donna*, September 1967, p. 124

The same bib necklace photographed
before on Rossana Schiaffino, c.1967
Swarovski "Margarita" crystals mounted
on a weft of transparent half-crystal beads
Marked: Made in Italy by Coppola e Toppo

The same eye mask as photographed
below on Rossana Schiaffino, c.1967
Swarovski "Margarita" crystals fixed on a weft-
mounted plastic transparent beaded sheath
containing a wooden rod

Rosanna Schiaffino wearing a Coppola e Toppo eye mask
in *Oggi*, February 20th 1968, p.45 (photographer unknown)

Isa Stoppi wearing Coppola e Toppo earrings
photographed by Gian Paolo Barbieri for *Linea
Italiana*, spring-summer 1967, unnumbered
Mila Schön/Gandini advertising page

Isa Stoppi wearing Coppola e Toppo earrings photographed by Gian Paolo Barbieri for *Linea Italiana*, spring-summer 1977, unnumbered Mila Schön/Terragni advertising page

Necklace with three festoons shaped as branches
with leaf motifs made for Valentino, 1968
Small gilded aluminium tubes and *roses montées* fixed to
an underlying weft of gilded glass faceted beads
Marked: Made in Italy by Coppola e Toppo
Published in Italian *Vogue*, September 1968, p.237 and
in an unnumbered Valentino advertising insert

Model wearing Coppola e Toppo jewellery, 1968
photographed by Gian Paolo Barbieri for a Valentino
advertising campaign in Italian *Vogue*, September 1968,
unnumbered page

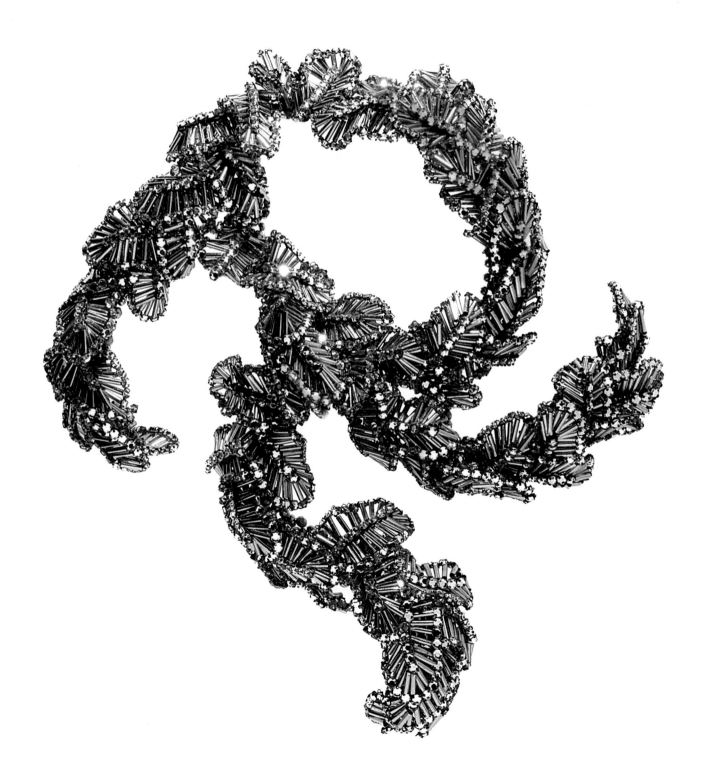

Pochette made for Valentino, c.1967
Pressed leather imitating alligator skin with 'V'
for Valentino decorative motif in gilded metal
Signed: Coppola e Toppo per Valentino
Mania Hruska Collection, Milan

Twin-handle bag made for Valentino, c.1968
Alligator skin and gilded metal chain handles
Signed: Coppola e Toppo per Valentino
Private Collection, Milan

Handbag made for Valentino, 1967
Alligator skin and triangular-shaped
rigid gilded metal handles
Signed: Coppola e Toppo for Valentino
Published in *Oakland Tribune*, 5 October 1967
Private Collection, Milan

Jacqueline Kennedy Onassis carrying a Coppola e Toppo *pochette* at the Metropolitan Opera House in 1975
Photographed by Tom Wargacki, 1975
Tom Wargacki/WireImage/Getty Images

Nearly thirty years later, Caroline Kennedy (with Ed Schlossberg) was photographed carrying a Coppola e Toppo *pochette* at the "Jacqueline Kennedy: The White House Years" Costume Institute Gala of the Metropolitan Museum in New York in 2001
Photographed by R.J. Capak, 2001
Tom Wargacki/WireImage/Getty Images

Pochette made for Valentino, 1967
Small gilded aluminium tubes and *roses montées*, gilded metal clasp
Published in *Women's Wear Daily*, 22 September 1967; also on a Valentino dress in *Linea Italiana* (Alta Moda), spring-summer 1968. This model also exists made from small anodised aluminium tubes in azure, red and various hues of brown
Pupa (Maria Cristina) Coppola Collection, Milan

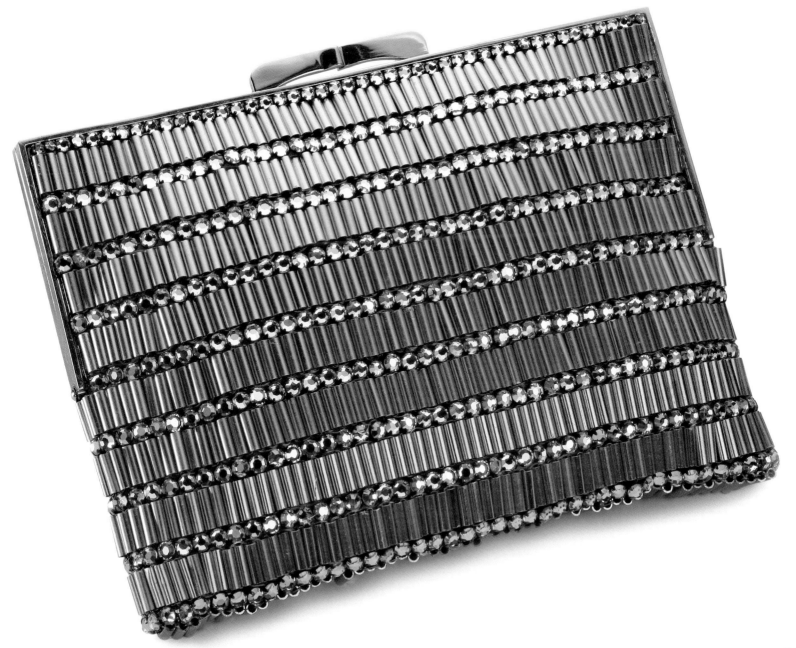

Belt and demi-parure made up of bracelet and
earrings made for Valentino, 1967
Blue, red and brown imitating tortoise-shell plastic
Right-hand set published in *Successo*, June 1967, p.139
Private Collection, Milan

Mirella Petteni wearing Coppola e Toppo earrings
and bracelet for an advertising campaign for
Valentino dresses made from Taroni fabric
photographed by Gian Paolo Barbieri
Published in *Linea Italiana*, spring-summer 1967,
unnumbered Valentino/Taroni advertising page

Mirella Petteni wearing Coppola e Toppo
earrings and holding a belt/necklace for an
advertising campaign for Valentino dresses
made from Taroni fabric
photographed by Gian Paolo Barbieri
Published in *Linea Italiana*, spring-summer 1967,
unnumbered Valentino/Taroni advertising page

Cuff bracelet made for Valentino, 1967
Small glass tubes and embroidered square-cut rhinestones
Published in *Women's Wear Daily*, 21 July 1967 and in
Linea Italiana, autumn-winter 1967-68, p. 159
Donatella Pellini Collection, Milan

Necklace with earrings made for Valentino, 1967
Small gilded aluminium tubes painted in two hues of brown
and *roses montées*
Marked: Made in Italy by Coppola e Toppo
The necklace is identical to the one that belonged to Jacqueline Kennedy,
sold at the Sotheby's auction in New York, 24-25 April 1996, lot 508, at
$18.400 plus the rights
Published in *Women's Wear Daily*, 15 September 1967

Mirella Petteni wearing two necklaces one on top
of the other by Coppola e Toppo for Valentino
photographed by Gian Paolo Barbieri for *Linea Italiana*,
autumn/winter 1967-68
One of the images shot on this occasion appears on the
magazine cover

Thong (flip-flop) sandals, second half of the 1960s
Silvery leather, Swarovski "Margarita" crystals,
plastic faceted beads

**Sling-back sandals made for Guido Pasquali,
second half of the 1960s**
Metallised shocking pink-painted leather, Swarovski
rectangular rhinestones

Sling-back sandals made for Emilio Pucci,
second half of the 1960s
Natural leather and string and weft-
mounted multicoloured faceted beads
Unger Collection, Milan

Page 232: Thong (flip-flop) sandal, c.1968
photographed by Gian Paolo Barbieri
Multicoloured plastic beads

Page 233: Isa Stoppi wearing the
Coppola e Toppo "Cotta" bikini
photographed by Gian Paolo Barbieri
for *Panorama*, 18 May 1968, p.49

Page 234: Mirella Petteni wearing
the Coppola e Toppo "Trikini"
photographed by Gian Paolo Barbieri
for *Panorama*, 18 May 1968, p.49

Page 235: Isa Stoppi wearing the
Coppola e Toppo "Crociata" bikini
photographed by Gian Paolo Barbieri
for *Panorama*, 18 May 1968, p.49

Mirella Petteni wearing a pair of Coppola
e Toppo dangling earrings
photographed by Gian Paolo Barbieri for *Linea
Italiana*, autumn-winter 1966-67, p. 51

Demi-parure made up of "Fireworks" choker
and bracelet, 1968
Embroidery disks in half-crystal fixed on the tip of annealed
wire segments forming a radial pattern, each segment is
mounted to an underlying weft of transparent crystals
Marked on clasp: Made in Italy by Coppola e Toppo
Necklace published in Italian *Vogue*, September 1968, p.240
A 'demi-parure' made up of this necklace and two bracelets
was sold at the Doyle auction in New York on April 11th 2006,
lot 210, at $11,400 plus the rights
Barbara Berger Collection, Mexico City

Page 238: Mirella Petteni wearing a Coppola
e Toppo hair ornament made with the same
technique as the "Fireworks" necklace
photographed by Gian Paolo Barbieri for Italian *Vogue*,
September 1968, p.313

Page 239: Cinzia Corman wearing the Coppola
e Toppo "Fireworks" necklace
photographed by Gian Paolo Barbieri for
Italian *Vogue*, September 1968, p.229

Carolina Alvarado Camero wearing the "Fireworks"
choker, March 2006

Three-strand necklace and wrapping bracelet made for Valentino, 1969
Bracelet made up of plastic cabochons surrounded by gilded metal spheres
fixed on an underlying beaded sheath covering a memory wire
Necklace made up of plastic central cabochons surrounded by gilded metal
spheres and string mounted coral-coloured painted glass beads
Bracelet and necklace both marked: Made In Italy by Coppola e Toppo
Published in *Linea Italiana*, spring-summer 1969, pp.156-157

Ivana Bastianello wearing a belt for
Valentino, 1969
photographed by Gian Paolo Barbieri
for Italian *Vogue*, March 1969, p.263

Demi-parure made up of collar necklace and earrings made for Valentino, 1969
Cabochon-cut plastic imitating turquoise alternating with set rectangular rhinestones, both mounted on an underlying weft of transparent plastic faceted beads
Marked: Made in Italy by Coppola e Toppo

Cuff bracelet for Valentino, 1969
Small gilded aluminium tubes and set rectangular rhinestones
fixed on an underlying weft of gilded glass beads
Marked: Made in Italy by Coppola e Toppo
Published in *Linea Italiana*, autumn/winter 1969/1970, p.131
Belts made with the same technique as the bracelet were
published in Italian *Vogue*, December 1968, p.98
Leila Marzagao Collection, London

Ivana Bastianello wearing a Coppola e Toppo
necklace For Valentino
photographed by Gian Paolo Barbieri for Italian
Vogue, March 1969, p.335

Lola Revedin wearing Coppola e Toppo gloves
photographed by Gian Paolo Barbieri, c.1967
The same gloves were published in American *Vogue*,
June 1967, p.106

Belt with buckle forming a removable cigarette case, c.1971
Leather belt, buckle base and cigarette case in silver plated metal
externally and gilded metal internally
Marked on buckle: Made in Italy by Coppola e Toppo
Gian Paolo Barbieri Collection, Milan

Leather base and brass cast lid with lunar surface look
Label inside the box: Coppola Toppo Milano
Gian Paolo Barbieri Collection, Milan

Silk scarf printed with photo of the lunar surface, c.1970
Signed: Coppola e Toppo
Enrico Quinto Collection, Rome

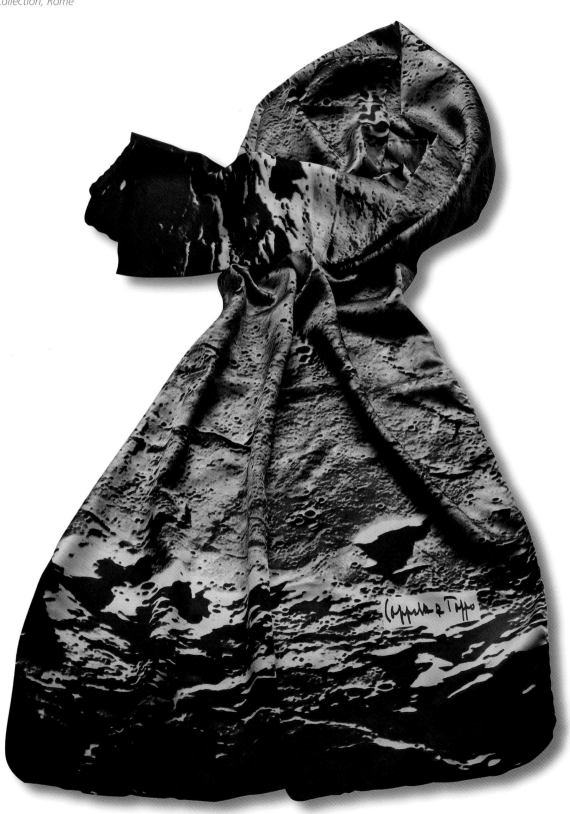

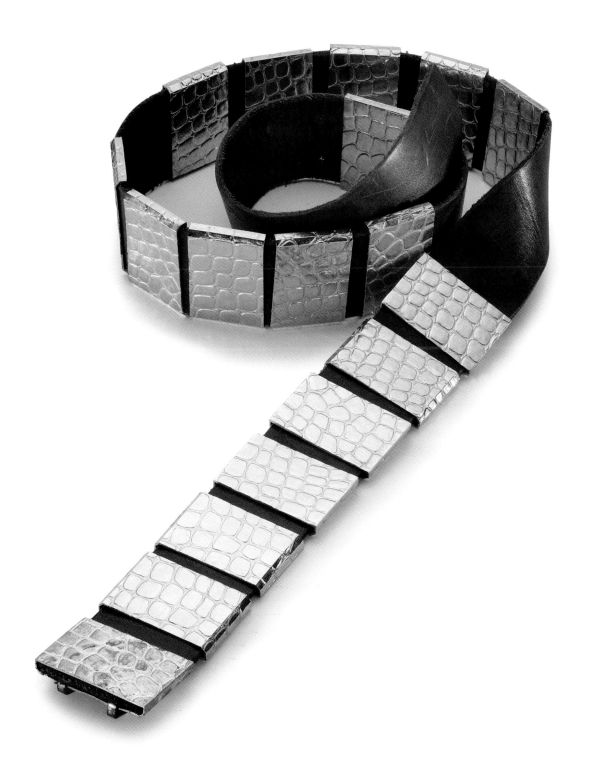

Belt, c.1970
Leather and gilded metal pressed with
motifs simulating the lunar surface
Gian Paolo Barbieri Collection, Milan

Demi-parure made up of brooch and earrings
made for Valentino, 1969
Plastic parallelepiped in the centre surrounded by
mountings containing 'baguettes' cut rhinestones
fixed to the underlying metal beading screen
Marked: Made in Italy by Coppola e Toppo
A belt made with the same elements was published
in *Harper's Bazaar*, October 1969, p.261

Four-strand bracelet with plastic centre made for Valentino, 1969
String mounted glass paste spheres simulating lapis lazuli and parallelepiped plastic in the centre surrounded by mountings containing baguette-cut rhinestones fixed to the underlying metal beading screen, conterie
A belt made with the same decorative central element was published in *Harper's Bazaar*, October 1969, p.261

Page 256: Veruschka wearing a Coppola e Toppo body ornament
photographed by Gian Paolo Barbieri for Italian *Vogue*, June 1975, p.53

Page 257: Berkley Johnson wearing a Coppola e Toppo body ornament
photographed by Gian Paolo Barbieri, 1969

Choker necklace made for Valentino, 1969
Double rhinestone chain containing baguette-cut
rhinestones, brass clasp with a semi-sphere in
faceted crystal surrounded by *roses montées*
A bracelet from the same collection was published
in *Linea Italiana*, autumn-winter 1969-70, p.88
Marked on clasp: Made in Italy by Coppola e Toppo
Donatella Pellini Collection, Milan

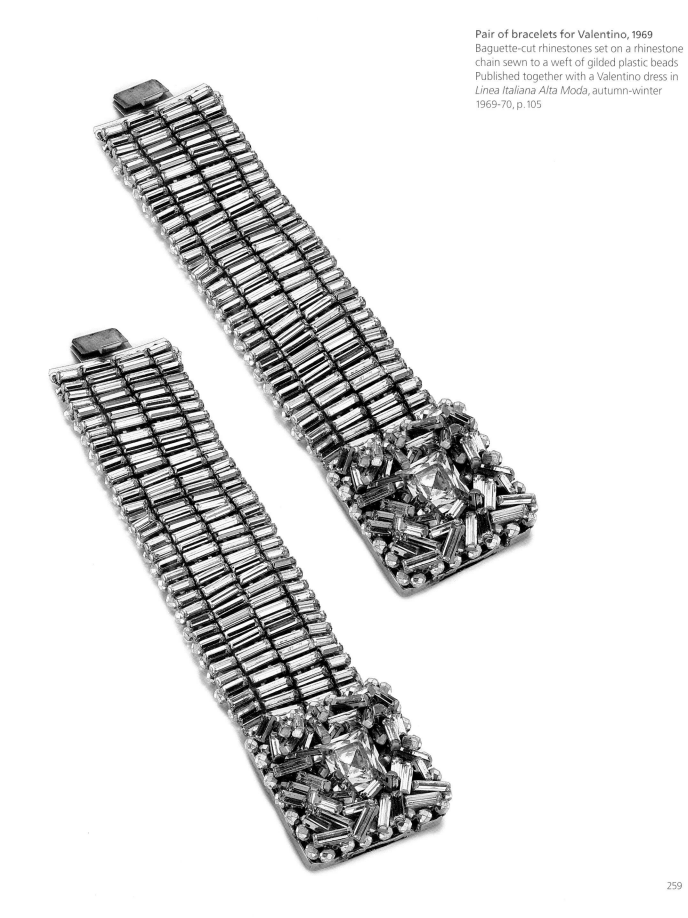

Pair of bracelets for Valentino, 1969
Baguette-cut rhinestones set on a rhinestone
chain sewn to a weft of gilded plastic beads
Published together with a Valentino dress in
Linea Italiana Alta Moda, autumn-winter
1969-70, p.105

Belt buckle and button earrings, 1969
Pyramid-style carré-cut grey plastic simulating
mother-of-pearl glued to gilded metal grille support
Earrings published in *Linea Italiana*,
autumn-winter 1969-70, p.88

**Belt made for Valentino,
autumn/winter collection 1968-69**
Gilded metal grate containing mother-of-
pearl rectangles is glued to a leather base
Gian Paolo Barbieri Collection, Milan

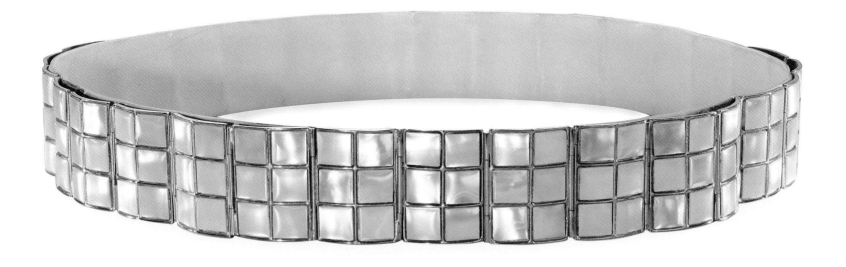

Demi-parure made up of two brooches and earrings for Valentino, 1970
Pierced gilded metal mountings containing rectangular rhinestones sewn within gilded metal pierced bars
In the earrings *roses montées* mounted in a circle going around a silver plated metal semi-sphere with set rectangular rhinestones simulating emeralds
Marked: Made in Italy by Coppola e Toppo

Demi-parure made up of a brooch and earrings for Valentino, 1970
Silver plated metal mountings containing rectangular rhinestones placed side by side and *roses montées* on the edges
Marked: Made in Italy by Coppola e Toppo

Demi-parure made up of an Egyptian
style necklace and earrings made for
Valentino, 1970
Gilded metal mountings containing
rectangular rhinestones placed side by
side and on the edges *roses montées*
Marked: Made in Italy by Coppola e Toppo

Five-strand necklace, 1970
String-mounted coral-coloured plastic tubes,
gilded plastic balls
Marked on gilded metal clasp: Coppola Toppo

Scarf necklace, c.1970
String-mounted half-crystal faceted beads
and interspersed by small coral branches
in the final tassel

265

Page 266: Ivana Bastianello wearing
a Coppola e Toppo choker
photographed by Gian Paolo Barbieri
for an advert, c.1970

Page 267: Berkley Johnson wearing
a Coppola e Toppo necklace
photographed by Gian Paolo Barbieri
for an advert, c.1970

Collar necklace for Valentino, 1970
Black plastic spheres and tortoiseshell-like semi-spheres marked with gilded polyethylene rings
Anna Negrisoli Bellora Collection, Milan

Single-strand necklace, 1972
Gilded metal spheres and wood segments
Marked on clasp: Coppola
Published in Italian *Vogue* on a Titti
Brugnoli outfit, March 1972, p. 195
Private Collection, Milan

Choker, c.1970
Gilded metal chain and brown plastic
plates imitating tortoiseshell
Marked on clasp: Coppola Toppo

Choker, c.1971
Gilded brushed metal bars and
pure crystal faceted beads
Marked on clasp: Coppola Toppo

Three-strand necklace with central
circular motif made for Ken Scott, 1971
Graduated painted coral-coloured glass
spheres, metal base centre overlapped by a
plastic semi-sphere surrounded by rectangular
set rhinestones and *roses montées*
Marked: Made in Italy by Coppola e Toppo
Shown on a Ken Scott dress in Italian *Vogue*,
April 1971, p.276

Demi-parure made up of necklace with central
pendant and earrings made for Valentino, 1971
Rectangular rhinestones set and mounted forming
a strand terminating in a central floral motif made
up of a plastic semi-sphere in the centre surrounded
by rectangular set rhinestones
Donatella Pellini Collection, Milan

Christiana Steidten wearing a Coppola e Toppo brooch
photographed by Gian Paolo Barbieri for a Valentino advertising
insert published in Italian *Vogue*, October 1973, unnumbered page

Christiana Steidten wearing a Coppola e Toppo brooch
photographed by Gian Paolo Barbieri for a Valentino advertising
insert published in Italian *Vogue*, October 1973, unnumbered page

Veruschka wearing Coppola e Toppo fashion jewellery
photographed by Gian Paolo Barbieri for Italian *Vogue*,
June 1975, pp.50-51

Dayle Haddon wearing Coppola e Toppo
jewels, Santa Margherita, 1975
photographed by Gian Paolo Barbieri

Headphone/jewel by Coppola e Toppo
photographed by Gian Paolo Barbieri
for Italian *Vogue*, February 1976, p.110

Headphone/jewel by Coppola e Toppo
photographed by Gian Paolo Barbieri
for Italian *Vogue*, February 1976, p.102

Definitive information on the possible dates corresponding to the hallmarks adopted along the years by Coppola e Toppo is scarce. Below is a listing detailing all the currently available information:

UNSIGNED Several pieces of fashion jewellery that were part of the collection that appeared in 1949 in French *Vogue* were not marked. We can therefore deduce that the very first Coppola e Toppo production runs might be unsigned.

The signature is also missing in those pieces that have no support on which to engrave a mark (for example those entirely made of weft-mounted crystal beads or glass paste spheres).

All the pieces in this book that do not have a mark mentioned in the caption are unsigned.

MIKY (a) To the information given above about the first Coppola e Toppo production, it should be added that the orders by Jacques Fath and Elsa Schiaparelli in 1949 written on their company-headed paper carry the wording "Micky de Coppola et Toppo": this would suggest that Miky was the first mark engraved on some pieces dated 1949 and 1950, as can be seen from the necklace that was part of the collection photographed for the article in American *Vogue* dated 1 November, 1949 (see p.71)

MADE IN ITALY BY COPPOLA E TOPPO (b) In different years, I traced two specimens of a Coppola e Toppo bracelet for Schiaparelli photographed in 1952 for French *Vogue*, both with the mark "Made in Italy by Coppola e Toppo". The same signature appears on the necklace photographed on the cover of French *Vogue* in May 1951, (see p.31). This evidently demonstrates that this mark was being used in 1951 and continued to be used till the beginning of 1960, when it was replaced by "Coppola e Toppo".

C ᴇ T (c), MADE ITALY C ᴇ T (d), C ᴇ T MADE IN ITALY (e) Dating Coppola e Toppo marks is made even more complicated when one notes that the necklace on page 33, a chromatic variation of the necklace for Schiaparelli published in French *Vogue* (p.76, May 1951) is signed "C e T Made Italy", while the bracelet (p.50) is stamped "C e T". This leads one to think that there were at least four marks being used in the same years: "C e T" (probably for the Italian market), as well as "Made Italy CᴇT" "Made in Italy by Coppola ᴇ Toppo" and "C ᴇ T Made in Italy" for the foreign markets.

COPPOLA TOPPO (f) Almost all the pieces made after 1960, including the models from the previous years remade in different colours to suit the gaudy range of the 1960s, carry the mark "Coppola Toppo", and this therefore, most probably, is the mark that characterised the production of that decade.

(a)

(b)

(c)

(d)

(e)

(f)

OTHER MARKS ON WHICH THERE IS NO PRECISE INFORMATION Of all the other marks adopted by Coppola e Toppo ("Made Italy", "Made in Italy", "CT", "CT Made Italy", "CᴇT", "Made in Italy CᴇT", "Coppola Toppo" engraved on oval metal plates, "Coppola e Toppo" embossed on gilded cardboard), there is no precise information with regard to their date of implementation. I have assigned approximate dates by means of deduction.

As the expression "Made Italy" (g) in English is ungrammatical and the fashion jewels stamped with this trademark are very simple and characterized by the use of pure crystal and half-crystal beads in the same object, we can reasonably assume that this mark was adopted at the start of the Coppola e Toppo business (1950) and then corrected to "Made in Italy" (h) from 1951 onwards.

CT Considering that the inscription in italics "*CT*" (i) and "*CT* Made Italy" is stylish but a little antiquated compared to the same inscription in block capitals and that the fashion jewels stamped with this trademark in italics are rather "primitive", I have come to the conclusion that these two marks must have been the first to be adopted after "Miky"; "*CT*" for the Italian market, "*CT* Made Italy" for the foreign markets, later converted into "C ᴇ T" and "Made in Italy CᴇT" as mentioned above.

The oval metal plates and the gilded cardboard with the inscription "Coppola Toppo" were certainly adopted in the 1960s.

Dating Coppola e Toppo jewels is made even more complicated by the fact that the metal plates (clasps and rigid ornamental structures) already stamped with a mark rather than another, were used over the years on the basis of their suitability for a certain model of jewel, regardless of whether or not the mark coincided with the one normally used during that period.

We can therefore conclude that the dating of each Coppola e Toppo jewel should be based on its style rather than on the mark inscribed on the piece. The choice of colours, the use of certain materials, the dimensions, all provide more information for reliable dating than the marks stamped on the metal plates.

Last but not least, we have also noted that, quite often, the oval metal plates engraved with the inscription "Coppola Toppo" and the gilded cardboard with the same embossed trademark are applied on jewels that are not original Coppola e Toppo creations.

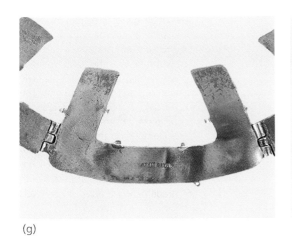

(g)

(h)

(i)

Books

Alfonsi, M. V., *I grandi personaggi della moda*, Cappelli Editori, Bologna, 1974

Becker, V., *Fabulous Fakes,* Grafton Books, Victoria, 1988

Bianchino, G., Quintavalle A. C., *Moda dalla fiaba al design – Italia 1951 – 89,* De Agostini, Novara, 1989

Bottero, A., *Nostra signora la moda,* Mursia, Milan, 1979

Butazzi, G. and Molfino, A.M., *La Moda Italiana,* (two volumes), Electa, Milan, 1987

Cosi, M., *Valentino che veste di nuovo,* Camunia, Brescia, 1984

de Cerval, M. (ed.), *Dictionnaire International du bijou*, Éditions du Regard, Paris, 1998

Farneti Cera, D. (ed.), *Jewels of fantasy- Costume jewelry of the 20th Century*, Harry N. Abrams, New York, 1992

Farneti Cera, D., *Costume Jewelry*, Antique Collectors' Club, Suffolk, 1997

Fiorentini Capitani, A., *Moda Italiana anni cinquanta e sessanta*, Cantini, Florence, 1991

Giacomoni, S., *L'Italia dell'Alta Moda,* Gabriele Mazzotta, Milan, 1984

Giordani, A. B. (ed.), *Il disegno dell'alta moda italiana 1940 – 70,* De Luca, Rome, 1982

Gordon, A., *Twentieth Century Costume Jewellery*, Adasia International, Hong Kong, 1990

Martin, R., *American Ingenuity. Sportswear 1930s – 1970s,* exhibition catalogue, Metropolitan Museum, New York, 2 April-16 August 1998

Morini, E., 'La Semplice, Meravigliosa Moda Italiana' in *Anni Cinquanta – La nascita della creatività italiana,* ['The simple, wonderful Italian fashion' in *The fifties – the birth of Italian creativity*] exhibition catalogue, Palazzo Reale, Milano, 4 March-3 July 3, 2005, Skira, Milan, 2005

Morini, E., *Storia della moda XVIII – XX secolo,* Skira, Milan, 2006

Moro, G., *European Designer Jewelry,* Schiffer Publishing, Atglen, PA., 1995

Müller, F., *Costume Jewellery for Haute Couture,* Thames & Hudson, London, 2006

Quinto, E. and Tinarelli, P., *Un secolo di moda*, Federico Motta, Milan, 2003

Ricci, S., 'La donazione Emilio Pucci: colore e fantasia', in *La galleria del Costume informa* n. 5, ['The Emilio Pucci donation: colour and imagination' in *Costume gallery information No.5*], exhibition catalogue, Palazzo Pitti, Florence, December-April, 1993

Soli, P., *Il genio antipatico – creatività e tecnologia della moda italiana 1951/1983,* Mondadori, Milan, 1984

Vergani, G., *La sala bianca – nascita della moda italiana,* Electa, Milan, 1992

Vergani, G., *Maria Pezzi – una vita dentro la moda,* Skira, Milan, 1998

Magazines

American *Vogue* 1949 – 1973

American *Harper's Bazaar* 1950 – 1972

Linea and *Linea Italiana* 1965 – 1975

Novità 1950 – 1965

Vogue Italia 1965 – 1975